CYRUS
THE GREAT

*The Rise of the Persian Empire
and the Legacy of
Ancient Persia's Greatest King*

SAMUEL CORWIN

Table of Contents

Introduction
The Problem with Cyrus the Great

He freed the slaves, respected the gods of his enemies, and built an empire stretching from the Aegean to the borders of India - and yet almost everything we think we know about him may be wrong.

Cyrus the Great is one of the most celebrated figures in the ancient world. He appears in the Hebrew Bible as a messiah figure, anointed by God to free the Jewish people from Babylonian captivity. He inspired Alexander the Great, who reportedly wept at his tomb. Thomas Jefferson owned two copies of the *Cyropaedia*, a Greek account of his life, and drew on its portrait of enlightened leadership when shaping his own political philosophy. For more than two and a half millennia, Cyrus has served as the ancient world's gold standard for what a ruler should be: powerful, just, and merciful.

But here is the problem. Nearly every source we have about Cyrus was written by someone who wanted something from him - or from his memory. The Hebrew scribes who praised him needed a liberator. The Greek historians who chronicled him needed a foil for their own political arguments. The Babylonian priests who welcomed him into their city needed a legitimate king. And Cyrus himself, or at least his court, produced propaganda designed to cement his divine mandate. Strip away the flattery, the mythology, and the political convenience, and what remains?

That is the question this book sets out to answer.

Why Cyrus Still Matters

Few figures from the ancient world have cast as long a shadow. Cyrus conquered Babylon in 539 BCE, an event so significant that it reshaped the political map of the entire Near East in a single campaign season. He absorbed the territories of Media, Lydia, and the Neo-Babylonian Empire into a single administrative structure - the Achaemenid Empire - that would endure, in various forms, for two centuries after his death.

But his influence is not merely territorial. Cyrus became a template. A model. A name invoked across cultures and centuries whenever someone wanted to argue that power and virtue could coexist. Iranian nationalists have claimed him. Human rights advocates have cited the Cyrus Cylinder - a clay barrel inscription discovered in the ruins of Babylon - as the world's first charter of human rights. American founding fathers studied his leadership. Modern leaders from across the political spectrum have found in Cyrus whatever they needed to find.

That is precisely what makes him so difficult to study honestly.

When a historical figure becomes a symbol, the symbol tends to swallow the person. We stop asking what Cyrus actually did and start asking what we want him to mean. This book resists that temptation. It takes Cyrus seriously enough to treat him as a human being - ambitious, strategic, sometimes brutal, and operating within a world of competing powers, fragile alliances, and ancient religious politics - rather than as an icon waiting to be borrowed.

He matters because he was real. And the real story is more interesting than the legend.

The Mystery of Cyrus: Conflicting Sources

Every serious student of Cyrus eventually runs into the same wall: the sources contradict each other, and none of them are neutral.

Take the question of his origins. Herodotus, writing in the fifth century BCE, gives us a dramatic birth narrative involving prophecy, royal intrigue, and a child left to die on a hillside. According to this account, Cyrus was the son of Cambyses I - described variously as a

Persian king or simply a man of good Persian family - and Mandane, the daughter of the Median king Astyages. Astyages, warned by a dream that his grandson would one day overthrow him, ordered the infant Cyrus killed. The child survived, was raised by a herdsman, and eventually fulfilled the prophecy. It is a compelling story. It also bears a striking resemblance to other ancient tales of hidden royal heirs - Moses in the bulrushes, Romulus and Remus exposed on the riverbank.

Did it happen? Almost certainly not in the way Herodotus tells it. But that does not mean it is useless. Myths about origins reveal what later generations believed - or needed to believe - about a figure's destiny and legitimacy.

Then there is the Cyrus Cylinder itself, often cited as evidence of his enlightened rule. Discovered in 1879 in the ruins of Babylon, the inscription presents Cyrus as the chosen servant of Marduk, the chief Babylonian deity, sent to restore proper worship after the impious reign of Nabonidus - the last ruler of the Neo-Babylonian Empire, who had alienated the powerful Babylonian priesthood by neglecting Marduk's cult. The cylinder describes Cyrus entering Babylon peacefully, freeing captive peoples, and allowing exiled communities to return to their homelands.

It is a remarkable document. It is also royal propaganda.

This does not make it false, but it demands careful reading. The cylinder was almost certainly composed by Babylonian priests, not by Cyrus personally. It served the interests of both the new Persian king and the religious establishment that had just handed him the city. Herodotus, meanwhile, emphasizes a very different kind of resourcefulness: he describes Cyrus diverting the Euphrates River during the Babylonian campaign to allow his troops to enter the city through the riverbed - an engineering feat that speaks more to military cunning than to divine favor.

Which version is true? Possibly both, in different ways. Possibly neither, in the ways they claim. Historians differ on the precise sequence of events surrounding the fall of Babylon, and the honest answer is that the sources do not fully agree. What they do agree on is the outcome: by 539 BCE, Cyrus controlled Babylon, and the world had changed.

The Problem with Existing Books

Given how much has been written about Cyrus, one might reasonably ask whether another book is necessary. The answer depends on what you think the existing books get wrong.

Most popular accounts of Cyrus fall into one of two traps. The first is uncritical admiration - treating the ancient sources at face value, reproducing the legend of the benevolent liberator without adequately interrogating the interests behind that legend. These books give us a Cyrus who is almost too good to be true, because their sources were designed to make him seem that way.

The second trap is the opposite: a kind of revisionist skepticism that dismisses the positive accounts entirely and reduces Cyrus to just another ancient conqueror, no different from the Assyrian kings who deported entire populations or the Babylonian rulers who razed cities. This approach corrects one distortion by introducing another.

Both approaches miss what is genuinely fascinating about Cyrus: the tension between the image and the reality, and what that tension tells us about how power works. Cyrus was not a saint. His campaigns involved real violence, real displacement, and real coercion. His unsuccessful campaign against the Massagetae in Scythia - the nomadic people of the eastern steppes - ended in his death and, by some accounts, his decapitation. That is not the ending of a myth. That is the ending of a man.

At the same time, his policies toward conquered peoples were genuinely different from those of his predecessors. Whether that difference was driven by moral conviction or political calculation - or both - is one of the questions worth taking seriously.

How This Book Is Different

This book does not set out to rescue Cyrus from his critics or to topple him from his pedestal. It sets out to understand him.

That means reading the sources carefully and skeptically - asking not just what they say but who wrote them, for whom, and why. It means treating the Cyrus Cylinder as a political document without dismissing what it reveals. It means taking Herodotus seriously as a historian while acknowledging his limitations. It means looking at Cyrus through multiple lenses: Persian, Babylonian, Hebrew, and Greek.

It also means being honest about what we do not know. The ancient world does not yield clean answers. Dates are disputed, accounts conflict, and the voices of ordinary people - the soldiers, the slaves, the farmers whose lives were upended by conquest - are almost entirely absent from the record. Where the evidence is thin, this book says so. Where historians disagree, it presents the disagreement rather than papering over it.

What emerges is a portrait of a figure who was genuinely extraordinary by the standards of his time - and genuinely human in all the ways that matter.

How to Read This Book

Each chapter focuses on a specific dimension of Cyrus's life and legacy: his origins and rise to power, his military campaigns, his administrative innovations, his treatment of conquered peoples, and the long afterlife of his reputation. The chapters can be read in sequence as a continuous narrative, or consulted individually as standalone explorations of particular themes.

Where primary sources are quoted or paraphrased, the context of those sources is explained. Where modern scholarly debate is relevant, it is acknowledged without turning the text into an academic argument. The goal throughout is clarity - not simplification, but the kind of honest plainness that respects both the complexity of the past and the intelligence of the reader.

Cyrus the Great lived and died more than 2,500 years ago. He left behind an empire, a legend, and a set of questions that historians are still arguing about. That argument is worth joining.

- Cyrus the Great conquered Babylon in 539 BCE and founded the Achaemenid Empire, one of the ancient world's largest political structures.

- His reputation as a benevolent ruler rests on sources - including the Hebrew Bible, the Cyrus Cylinder, and Greek histories - that each had their own political reasons to praise him.

- The Cyrus Cylinder, often cited as a proto-human rights document, was likely composed by Babylonian priests and served the interests of both Cyrus and the religious establishment.

- Accounts of Cyrus's origins vary significantly across ancient sources, reflecting the tendency to mythologize powerful figures rather than record them accurately.

- Herodotus and other Greek writers emphasized Cyrus's military ingenuity, including the alleged diversion of the Euphrates River during the Babylonian campaign.

- Cyrus died during an unsuccessful campaign against the Massagetae - a reminder that behind the legend was a mortal man operating in a dangerous world.

- This book approaches Cyrus by reading his sources critically, acknowledging historical uncertainty, and resisting both uncritical admiration and reflexive skepticism.

The legend of Cyrus has proven more durable than most empires. But legends, however powerful, are not the same as history - and the history, when you look at it closely, turns out to be stranger, richer, and more instructive than the myth. What follows is an attempt to find the man inside the monument.

Chapter 1
The Boy Who Was Meant to Die

A king dreamed of a vine. It grew from his daughter's womb and spread until it covered all of Asia. When he woke, he summoned his priests - and what they told him changed the course of history.

That dream belonged to Astyages, ruler of the Median Empire, one of the most powerful men in the ancient world. His priests interpreted it as a warning: a grandson would one day rise up and take everything from him. Astyages had a daughter named Mandane. He had plans for her. And when she gave birth to a son, the king made a decision that would haunt him for the rest of his life.

He ordered the child killed.

What followed - or what ancient sources tell us followed - is one of antiquity's great survival stories: a tale of prophecy defied, identity concealed, and power reclaimed. Whether every detail is literally true matters less than what the story reveals. The birth of Cyrus the Great was not merely a historical event. It was a myth that a civilization built itself upon, and the man at its center would go on to found the largest empire the world had yet seen.

Born Into the Wrong Family

Cyrus was born in Anshan, a region in Pars - the territory we now call Fars, in southwestern Iran. His exact birth date is lost to history, but his lineage is not. He was the son of Cambyses I, a Persian king who ruled Anshan as a vassal under Median authority, and Mandane, the daughter of Astyages himself. That made Cyrus both Persian and Median by blood - a detail that would later prove politically useful, but which, at the moment of his birth, made him dangerous.

The Median Empire was the dominant power across a vast stretch of the ancient Middle East. Persia was subordinate to it, a client kingdom that paid tribute and deferred to Median authority. Astyages had ruled since around 585 BCE, and his grip on the region was firm. But kings who rule by fear tend to see threats everywhere - and Astyages, it seems, was that kind of king.

When Mandane became pregnant, Astyages reportedly had a second dream. This time, a stream of water poured from his daughter's body and flooded the whole of Asia. His interpreters gave the same verdict: the child she carried would one day rule in his place.

Astyages had a choice. He could ignore the prophecy. He could wait and see. Instead, he acted.

The Order That Backfired

Astyages summoned one of his most trusted generals - a man named Harpagus - and gave him a direct command: take the infant and destroy it.

Harpagus was loyal, but he was also cautious. Killing a royal grandchild was not the kind of act a man could walk away from cleanly. If Astyages ever changed his mind, or if Mandane ever came to power, the general who had carried out the murder would be the first to pay. So Harpagus did what careful men in dangerous positions often do: he passed the responsibility to someone else.

He handed the child to a herdsman named Mitradates - or, in Herodotus's telling, a shepherd - with instructions to leave the infant exposed on a hillside to die. What happened next is where history and legend become genuinely difficult to separate.

According to the most famous version of the story, the shepherd could not bring himself to abandon the child. His wife had recently given birth to a stillborn baby, and together they made a decision: they would raise the living child as their own, and present the dead infant to Harpagus as proof the deed was done. Astyages was deceived. Harpagus was satisfied. And Cyrus - unknowing, unnamed, hidden among livestock and hills - grew up in the Median countryside as the son of a shepherd.

The Boy Who Couldn't Stay Hidden

The story of Cyrus's concealment has a turning point that feels almost theatrical. As a young boy, Cyrus was playing with other children in his village when he was chosen, in a game, to act as "king." He took the role seriously - perhaps too seriously. When one of the boys, the son of a Median nobleman, refused to obey him, Cyrus had him flogged.

The nobleman complained to Astyages. The king summoned the shepherd's son. And when Astyages looked at the boy standing before him, he saw something that unsettled him: a bearing, a confidence, a face that looked uncomfortably familiar.

He questioned Harpagus. The general, knowing he was caught, confessed. Astyages had been deceived for years. His grandson was alive.

What Astyages did next reveals the kind of ruler he was. Rather than acknowledge his own failure, he invited Harpagus to a banquet - and served him the flesh of his own son. It was a punishment designed to break a man's spirit entirely. Then, turning to the prophecy, Astyages consulted his priests again. They reassured him: the dream had already been fulfilled. The boy had been "king" in his game. The prophecy was spent.

Astyages chose to believe them. He sent Cyrus back to his birth parents in Anshan - to Cambyses and Mandane - and considered the matter closed.

He was wrong.

Youth, Return, and the Road to Anshan

Cyrus grew up in Anshan knowing who he was. He was a Persian prince, heir to a vassal kingdom, grandson of the man who had once tried to have him murdered. What he made of that knowledge, we can only infer. What we know is what he did with it.

By the time Cyrus came of age and rose to rule Anshan - likely sometime in the 550s BCE - he had inherited not just a title but a grievance, and a general with a score to settle. Harpagus, still nursing the wound of Astyages's monstrous revenge, had not forgotten what had been done to him. He began quietly working among the Median nobility, cultivating discontent, building the conditions for revolt.

When Cyrus declared his rebellion against Astyages, he did not do so alone. Harpagus defected to his side, bringing Median troops with him. The forces of Astyages crumbled. At the Battle of Pasargadae Hill, Cyrus's combined Persian and Median forces defeated the Median king. Astyages was captured - not killed, according to most accounts, but kept alive, a prisoner of the grandson he had once condemned to death.

The Median Empire fell. The Achaemenid Empire began.

What Herodotus Tells Us - and What He Doesn't

Nearly everything we know about Cyrus's early life comes from the Greek historian Herodotus, who wrote his *Histories* roughly a century after these events. Herodotus was a brilliant storyteller and a genuine researcher, but he was also working from oral traditions, Persian court narratives, and accounts that had already been shaped by decades of retelling.

He was aware of this. He noted that there were multiple versions of Cyrus's birth story in circulation and that he chose to present the one he found most credible. Other ancient sources - including the

Babylonian *Nabonidus Chronicle* and fragments of Ctesias of Cnidus - offer different details, though none contradict the basic arc of Cyrus's rise.

Historians today treat the shepherd narrative with measured skepticism. The broad strokes - Cyrus born of a Persian father and Median mother, raised in Anshan, eventually revolting against Astyages with Median support - are considered historically plausible. The prophecies, the dreams, the banquet of flesh: these carry the unmistakable signature of myth.

And that's not a flaw in the record. It's a feature of it.

The Myth That Made a King

Stories like Cyrus's were not unusual in the ancient world. They followed a pattern so consistent that the folklorist Otto Rank, writing in the early twentieth century, identified it as a recurring archetype: the hero of noble birth, abandoned or threatened in infancy, raised in obscurity, and eventually restored to his rightful place. Moses. Romulus. Oedipus. Sargon of Akkad, who preceded Cyrus by nearly two thousand years, had a nearly identical origin story - a mother who could not keep him, a basket, a river, a humble upbringing, a throne.

These stories were not accidental. They served a purpose.

In the ancient world, legitimate kingship required more than military victory. It required divine sanction - evidence that the gods had chosen this ruler, that his rise was not mere ambition but destiny. A king who survived a death sentence as an infant, who defied the most powerful man in the region through providence alone, was not just lucky. He was protected. He was chosen.

For Cyrus, the survival narrative did something else as well. It bridged two worlds. He was Persian by birth and Median by blood. His story explained, in terms any subject could understand, why a Persian king was also the legitimate heir to Median authority. He hadn't conquered the Medes - he had been born of them, hidden among them, and returned to them. The empire he built wasn't a foreign imposition. It was a homecoming.

How the Story Shaped the Man - and the Empire

Whether Cyrus himself believed the prophecy, promoted it, or simply allowed it to circulate, the effect was the same. His origin story became part of his political identity. It preceded him into conquered cities. It followed him into the historical record.

This matters because Cyrus would go on to govern in ways that were, by ancient standards, remarkably inclusive. He did not destroy the cultures he absorbed. He preserved temples, respected local customs, and allowed conquered peoples to maintain their traditions. Scholars have long debated how much of this was genuine philosophy and how much was shrewd statecraft - but the origin myth offers a clue. A king who was raised as one people and ruled as another had reason to understand that identity was not fixed, that legitimacy could be earned across boundaries, that empire could be built on something other than terror.

The boy who was meant to die became the man who built a world.

- Cyrus the Great was born in Anshan, Pars, to Cambyses I (a Persian king) and Mandane (daughter of the Median king Astyages), making him both Persian and Median by blood.

- Astyages ordered Cyrus killed at birth after interpreters warned him that his grandson would one day overthrow him.

- The general Harpagus, unwilling to carry out the murder directly, passed the infant to a shepherd, who raised Cyrus in secret.

- Astyages eventually discovered Cyrus was alive but was persuaded by his priests that the prophecy had already been fulfilled - a decision he would come to regret.

- Harpagus, punished savagely by Astyages, later defected to Cyrus and helped him defeat the Median forces at the Battle of Pasargadae Hill.

- The primary source for Cyrus's early life is Herodotus, writing roughly a century after the events; his account blends historical fact with mythological tradition.

- Cyrus's survival story follows a well-established ancient archetype - the hidden royal child - that served to legitimize his rule and bridge Persian and Median identities.

- His rise ended the Median Empire and established the Achaemenid Empire, one of the most consequential political transformations in ancient history.

Prophecies have a way of becoming self-fulfilling - not because the gods arrange it, but because people act on them. Astyages's fear of his grandson created the very conditions that produced his downfall: a resentful general, a hidden heir, and a revolt waiting for its moment. What began as a dream interpreted in a palace became an empire stretching across the ancient world.

The story of Cyrus's birth is where that empire starts. And it starts, as so many great things do, with someone trying very hard to prevent it.

15

Chapter 2
The Rebellion That Changed the World

A king who trusted his generals too much lost an empire. A grandson he tried to have killed built one instead.

That, in its most compressed form, is the story of how the Persian Empire was born - not through slow political evolution, but through a single, decisive act of rebellion that shattered the old order of the ancient Near East and replaced it with something the world had never quite seen before.

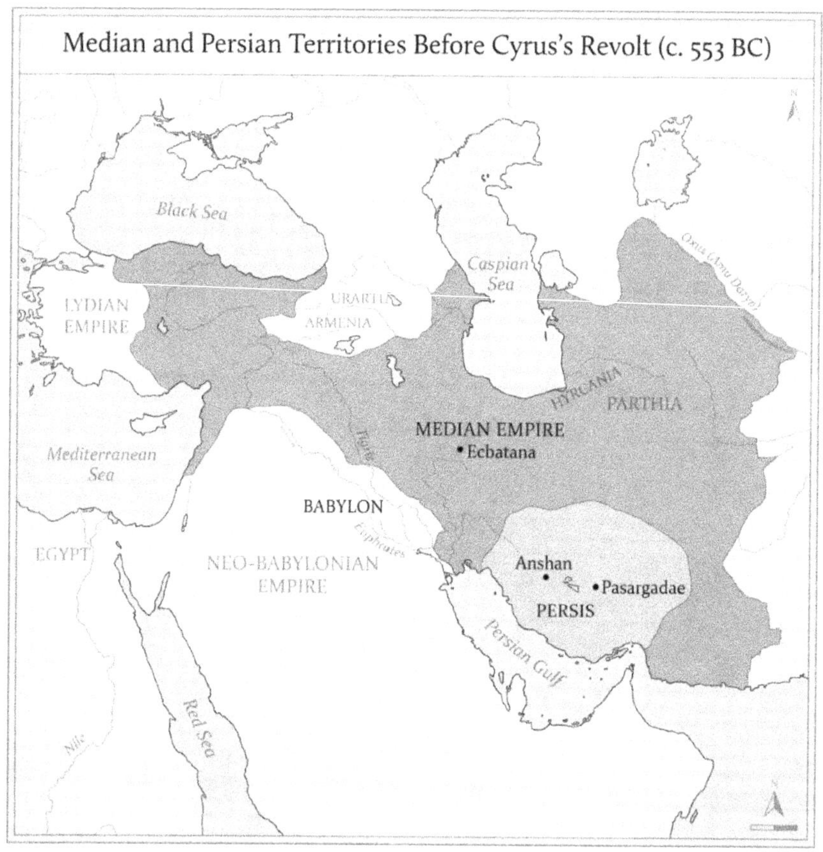

Median Empire vs Persian Territory (Pre-Rebellion)

By 553 BCE, the Median Empire had dominated the Iranian plateau for generations. Its capital, Ecbatana, sat high in the Zagros Mountains - a fortified city of layered walls and royal wealth, the seat of a power that stretched from Anatolia to the edges of Central Asia. The Medes had helped bring down the Assyrian Empire, carved up its territories, and established themselves as one of the great powers of the ancient world. They were, by any reasonable measure, unassailable.

Then Cyrus of Anshan decided otherwise.

What followed was more than a change of dynasty. It was a transformation of the political imagination of the ancient world - a demonstration that empires could be built not only on conquest and terror, but on something more durable: the loyalty of the conquered.

A Kingdom Under Median Shadow

To understand what Cyrus overthrew, you first have to understand what the Medes had built - and how they held it together.

Median rule over Persia was not the rule of a distant colonial power over a foreign people. The Persians and Medes shared deep cultural and linguistic roots, both being Iranian peoples who had migrated onto the plateau centuries earlier. What separated them was hierarchy, not ethnicity. The Medes sat at the top; the Persians, including the royal house of Anshan, occupied a subordinate but not entirely powerless position beneath them.

Cyrus's father, Cambyses, had ruled Anshan as a vassal king - a client monarch who owed his throne, at least in part, to Median tolerance. Anshan itself was a small kingdom in the region of Fars, in southwestern Iran. It was no backwater, but neither was it any rival to Ecbatana. The Persian kings of Anshan operated within a world defined by Median supremacy, and for a long time, that arrangement held.

Astyages, the Median king who would face Cyrus in rebellion, had ruled for decades. Ancient sources describe him as a man of considerable power but also considerable suspicion - a king haunted by prophecy and prone to the kind of cruelty that erodes loyalty over time. Whether those characterizations are entirely fair is a question historians have wrestled with, but the political reality they point to is clear: by the time Cyrus came of age, the foundations of Median authority were not as solid as they appeared.

Harpagus and the Seeds of Rebellion

No rebellion of this scale grows from a single grievance, and the revolt of Cyrus was no exception. What makes this particular uprising so historically vivid is the figure standing just behind Cyrus in the early stages - a Median general named Harpagus.

Harpagus was one of Astyages' most capable commanders, a man who had served the Median crown with distinction. He was also a man with a reason to want that crown destroyed.

According to Herodotus - our most detailed ancient source for these events - Astyages had once ordered Harpagus to expose and kill the infant Cyrus, whom the king feared would one day overthrow him based on a prophetic dream. Harpagus, unwilling to commit the act himself, passed the child to a herdsman who raised him in secret. When Astyages discovered the deception years later, his revenge was grotesque: he invited the general to a banquet and served him the flesh of his own son.

How much of this account is historical and how much is legend is genuinely uncertain. Herodotus was writing more than a century after these events, drawing on oral traditions and Persian court narratives that had their own political purposes. But the core dynamic the story captures - a powerful general with a personal vendetta against his king, willing to betray him at the critical moment - is historically plausible and consistent with what we know about how the rebellion unfolded.

When Cyrus raised his standard against Astyages around 553 BCE, Harpagus was waiting. He had, according to the ancient accounts, been in secret communication with Cyrus for some time, laying the groundwork for defection. He was not alone. Dissatisfaction within the Median military and aristocracy had been building, and Cyrus - young, charismatic, and presenting himself not as a foreign conqueror but as a legitimate ruler - offered a credible alternative.

Rebellions need a spark. They also need kindling. Harpagus was the kindling.

Cyrus Declares Revolt

When Cyrus formally declared revolt, he did so not merely as a Persian chieftain throwing off a foreign yoke, but as a king asserting a legitimate claim to rule. This distinction mattered enormously - both for how the rebellion was fought and for how it was remembered.

Cyrus was the fourth king of Anshan in his line, and he understood that legitimacy was as powerful a weapon as any army. His revolt was framed, at least in part, as a correction of Median overreach - a reassertion of proper order rather than a radical rupture. He cultivated the support of Persian tribes and clans who had chafed under Median dominance, presenting himself as their champion.

He also moved quickly. Speed was essential. A prolonged insurgency would give Astyages time to consolidate, to call in allies, to crush the rebellion before it could gather momentum. Cyrus understood that the window of opportunity - created by Median internal divisions and the treachery of Harpagus - would not stay open indefinitely.

The armies of Anshan were not, on paper, a match for the full military resources of the Median Empire. What Cyrus had instead was timing, internal support, and a general on the other side who was about to switch sides.

Key Battles and Turning Points

The war between Cyrus and Astyages was decided not by a single climactic engagement but by a sequence of confrontations in which military outcomes and political betrayals were inseparable.

The Battle of Pasargadae stands as the turning point. Astyages dispatched his army to meet the Persian rebellion, placing Harpagus in command - a decision that, in retrospect, looks like one of history's great miscalculations. At the critical moment, Harpagus defected, taking a substantial portion of the Median forces with him and delivering them to Cyrus.

The effect was devastating. An army that had marched out to crush a rebellion returned as part of one. Cyrus did not simply win the battle - he absorbed his enemy's military strength, transforming a potential defeat into a rout. Astyages, reportedly furious at the betrayal, executed the advisors who had counseled him to trust Harpagus. Then he personally led a second force against Cyrus.

That army, too, collapsed. Whether through further defections, outright defeat in the field, or some combination of both, Astyages' forces disintegrated. The Median king himself was captured - not killed, but taken prisoner.

Here Cyrus's character, or at least his political genius, becomes visible. He did not execute Astyages. He kept him alive, reportedly treating him with a degree of respect. This was not sentimentality. It was a signal - to the Median aristocracy, to the peoples of the empire, to anyone watching - that Cyrus was not a destroyer. He was a successor.

The Fall of Ecbatana

With Astyages in captivity and his armies broken, the road to Ecbatana lay open.

Cyrus marched on the Median capital and took it. The city that had been the heart of Median power for generations passed into Persian hands without, it seems, a prolonged siege or catastrophic destruction. Cyrus proclaimed himself ruler, and in doing so, he did not simply replace one king with another. He inherited the administrative structures, the court traditions, and the imperial networks that the Medes had built.

This was deliberate. Cyrus understood that destroying what he had conquered would leave him ruling rubble. Instead, he integrated Median institutions into his own emerging state, drawing on Median as well as Persian traditions to construct a new political identity. Median nobles were retained in positions of influence. Median customs were respected. The conquest was real, but it was wrapped in the language of continuity.

By the time the dust settled, the Achaemenid Empire had been born - named for Achaemenes, the legendary ancestor of Cyrus's royal line. It would grow, under Cyrus and his successors, into one of the largest empires the ancient world had ever seen.

What Historians Say

Sources on the Revolt

Our knowledge of these events rests on a foundation that is rich in narrative but uneven in reliability. Herodotus, writing in the fifth century BCE, provides the most detailed account of Cyrus's rise - including the dramatic story of Harpagus, the exposed infant, and the banquet of revenge. His *Histories* remain indispensable, but they were composed long after the events they describe, drawing on oral traditions and sources with their own agendas.

The *Nabonidus Chronicle*, a Babylonian cuneiform text, offers a more contemporary perspective on Cyrus's campaigns, though its focus is primarily on events in Mesopotamia rather than the earlier revolt against Astyages. Persian royal inscriptions, including the famous Cyrus Cylinder, provide Cyrus's own voice - or at least the voice of his court scribes - but these are propaganda documents as much as historical records.

Reliability and Contradictions

Historians differ on the degree to which Herodotus's account of the Cyrus-Astyages conflict can be trusted in its details. The story of the infant Cyrus, the prophetic dreams, and the banquet of Harpagus has the structure of folklore - a pattern of narrative that appears across cultures and eras. Many scholars treat these elements as legendary accretions around a historical core, rather than literal accounts.

What most historians do accept is the basic outline: Cyrus of Anshan rebelled against Astyages around 553 BCE, won a decisive military victory aided by defections within the Median army, captured Ecbatana, and established Persian supremacy over the Iranian plateau. The mechanisms of that victory - and the precise role of figures like Harpagus - remain subjects of ongoing scholarly discussion.

What It Means

Why Cyrus Won

Military victory rarely comes from military strength alone, and the revolt against Astyages illustrates this with unusual clarity. Cyrus won, in the first instance, because his enemy's army chose not to fight him. That choice was the product of years of accumulated grievance - against Astyages' cruelty, his poor judgment, his failure to maintain the loyalty of men like Harpagus.

But Cyrus also won because of what he offered. He presented himself as a ruler who would govern with restraint, who would respect existing institutions, who would not demand the humiliation of those who submitted to him. Whether this was genuine conviction or calculated policy - and it may well have been both - it worked. People defected to him, surrendered to him, and ultimately served him because the alternative seemed worse and the promise seemed real.

His mercy toward Astyages was not weakness. It was a demonstration, visible to everyone in the ancient Near East, of the kind of ruler he intended to be.

The Birth of the Persian Empire

What emerged from the rubble of Median power was something genuinely new. Cyrus did not simply inherit the Median Empire; he transformed it. By blending Persian and Median traditions, by incorporating rather than destroying the peoples he conquered, he laid the conceptual groundwork for an imperial model that would define the Achaemenid dynasty for two centuries.

That model - tolerant, administratively sophisticated, culturally inclusive - would reach its fullest expression in the decades ahead, as Cyrus pushed westward into Lydia and then south into Babylon. But its origins lay here, in the mountains of Iran, in the moment when a vassal king decided that the world could be arranged differently.

- Around 553 BCE, Cyrus of Anshan launched a rebellion against Astyages, the Median king who had dominated the Iranian plateau for generations.

- Cyrus's father, Cambyses, had ruled Anshan as a Median vassal; Cyrus transformed that subordinate kingdom into the nucleus of a new empire.

- Harpagus, a senior Median general with personal grievances against Astyages, defected to Cyrus at a critical moment, delivering much of the Median army and turning the tide of the war.

- At the Battle of Pasargadae, Cyrus defeated Astyages' forces; a second Median army, led personally by Astyages, also collapsed.

- Astyages was captured but not executed - a deliberate political signal that Cyrus intended to rule through integration, not destruction.

- Cyrus seized Ecbatana, the Median capital, and proclaimed himself ruler, blending Median and Persian traditions into a new imperial identity.

- Our primary sources - Herodotus, the *Nabonidus Chronicle*, and Persian royal inscriptions - are valuable but each carry their own limitations and biases.

- Cyrus's victory established the Achaemenid Empire, which would grow into one of the ancient world's largest and most influential political structures.

The rebellion of 553 BCE was, in one sense, a local affair - a vassal king throwing off the authority of his overlord in a mountainous corner of the ancient world. But the consequences rippled outward for centuries. Cyrus did not just win a war; he introduced a new way of thinking about what empire could mean. That idea - that power and mercy were not opposites, that conquered peoples could become willing subjects - would travel with his armies all the way to Babylon, and its echoes would reach far beyond the ancient world. What came next would prove just how far a single act of rebellion could carry.

Chapter 3
From King to Empire Builder

In 553 BCE, a Persian king named Cyrus raised his banner against the most powerful dynasty in the region - and almost no one expected him to win.

The Medes had dominated the ancient Near East for generations. Their empire stretched across what is now Iran and beyond, and Persia sat within their shadow, a subordinate kingdom paying tribute to a mightier overlord. Cyrus was a regional ruler, not a world-historical figure - not yet. What transformed him from one among many vassal kings into the founder of the largest empire the ancient world had seen was a combination of military audacity, political intelligence, and an approach to conquered peoples that was, by the standards of his age, almost startlingly humane.

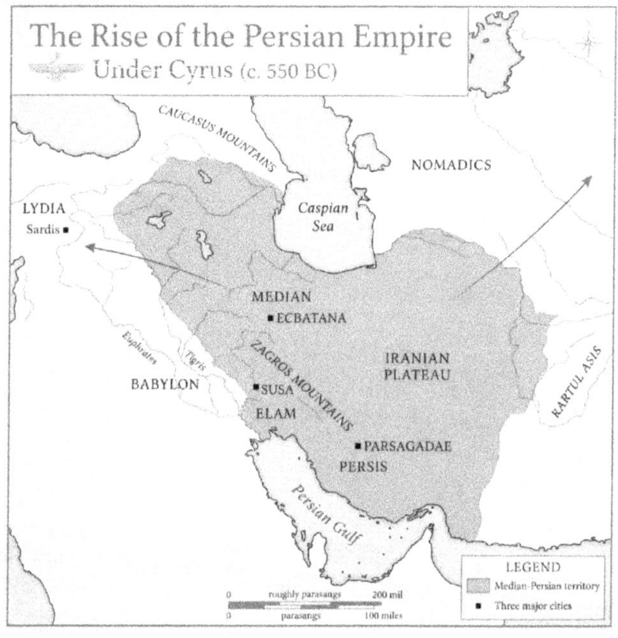

Early Expansion Map (Post-Media Conquest)

This chapter follows that transformation. It traces how Cyrus moved from rebellion against Median rule to the creation of a Persian Empire that would eventually stretch from the Aegean coast to the borders of India. It examines what we know - and what we don't - about the administrative machinery he built, and what his methods reveal about the kind of leader he was. His story is not simply one of conquest. It is a story about how empires are made: through force, yes, but also through persuasion, legitimacy, and the calculated generosity of a ruler who understood that winning a war and holding a kingdom are two very different problems.

Consolidating Power in Persia

When Cyrus launched his uprising against the Median dynasty in 553 BCE, he was not acting from a position of obvious strength. Persia was a client state. The Medes, under their king Astyages, held the dominant position in the region, and any rebellion against them was a serious gamble.

What followed over the next four years was a sustained military and political campaign that ended with Cyrus doing something remarkable: not simply defeating the Medes, but absorbing them. By 549 BCE, he had founded what would become the Achaemenid Persian Empire - named for the royal house from which he descended - and he did so by uniting the Medes and Persians rather than treating the Medes as a conquered enemy.

This was a deliberate choice, and it mattered enormously. Rather than dismantling Median institutions or humiliating Median elites, Cyrus incorporated them into his new imperial structure. Median nobles retained positions of influence. Median administrative practices were preserved and adapted. The result was not a Persian conquest of Media so much as a merger - unequal, certainly, but one that gave the defeated party a stake in the new order.

This pattern would define Cyrus's entire approach to empire-building. He was not interested in rubble. He was interested in functioning states that could be governed, taxed, and mobilized. Destruction was expensive. Integration was profitable.

Political Strategy and Alliances

With Median power broken and Persia consolidated, Cyrus turned his attention westward. In 547 BCE, he moved against Croesus, the King of Lydia - a figure so famously wealthy that his name became a byword for riches across the ancient world. Lydia occupied the western edge of Anatolia, roughly corresponding to the western portion of modern Turkey, and its capital at Sardis was one of the great cities of the age.

Croesus had reportedly misread an oracle's prophecy and believed a campaign against Persia would end in his favor. It did not. Cyrus captured Sardis and brought Lydia into the Persian orbit, extending his empire to the Aegean coast and placing him in direct contact - and eventual conflict - with the Greek world to the west.

What is striking about each of these campaigns is not just the military outcome but the political management that followed. Cyrus did not govern through terror alone. He cultivated legitimacy. He presented himself not as a foreign conqueror but as a rightful ruler - sometimes even as a liberator. This was not mere propaganda. It was a governing strategy, one that required him to understand the values, traditions, and grievances of the peoples he was absorbing.

Nowhere was this more visible than in Babylon.

Transition to Imperial Vision

In 539 BCE, Cyrus marched into Babylon - at that moment one of the most magnificent cities on earth, the capital of a Mesopotamian empire with roots stretching back millennia. Its fall to a Persian army might have meant looting, destruction, and the humiliation of its people. Under many conquerors of the ancient world, it would have.

Cyrus chose a different path. He entered Babylon not as a destroyer but as a restorer. He honored the city's gods, respected its temples, and presented himself as the legitimate successor to Babylonian kingship rather than its foreign usurper. Ancient inscriptions - most famously the Cyrus Cylinder, a clay document discovered in the nineteenth century - record his claims to have been chosen by the Babylonian god Marduk to rule the city and restore its sanctuaries.

Among those who responded most powerfully to his arrival were the Jewish communities living in Babylonian captivity. Deported from their homeland by the Babylonian king Nebuchadnezzar decades earlier, they found in Cyrus a ruler willing to allow their return to Judah and the rebuilding of their temple in Jerusalem. In the Hebrew Bible, Cyrus is described in terms reserved for few non-Israelite figures - as an instrument of divine purpose, a shepherd of God's people. That reception speaks volumes about how his rule was experienced by those who had suffered under his predecessors.

By this point, the Persian Empire encompassed an enormous swath of the ancient world: the territories of modern Iraq, Syria, Lebanon, and Israel, in addition to Persia, Media, and Lydia. Cyrus had built, in the span of roughly fourteen years, one of the largest political structures the ancient world had ever seen.

What Historians Say

Evidence of Early Administration

Reconstructing exactly how Cyrus organized his empire is not straightforward. The surviving evidence is fragmentary, drawn from a mix of Persian royal inscriptions, Babylonian administrative records, Greek historical accounts written generations after the fact, and biblical texts with their own theological purposes.

What the evidence does suggest is that Cyrus established a model of governance his successors would formalize and expand. The Achaemenid Empire would eventually be organized into provinces called satrapies, each governed by a satrap - a regional administrator who answered to the king. Whether Cyrus himself instituted this system in its full form or whether it developed under his immediate successors remains a matter of scholarly discussion. What seems clear is that the foundational logic - governing a vast, diverse empire through delegated regional authority rather than direct central control - was already present in his approach.

His treatment of Babylon offers the clearest administrative evidence. Rather than imposing a purely Persian governing apparatus, he worked within existing Babylonian structures, adapting them to Persian imperial purposes. This was pragmatic governance: it reduced resistance, preserved local expertise, and allowed the machinery of taxation and administration to keep running without interruption.

Gaps in Historical Records

Honest engagement with Cyrus's story requires acknowledging what we simply do not know. Much of what has been written about him - including by ancient authors - reflects the perspectives of people who admired him, feared him, or had theological reasons to portray him in a particular light. Greek historians like Herodotus wrote about Cyrus with a mixture of fascination and distance, sometimes preserving genuine historical memory and sometimes embellishing it with legend.

The Cyrus Cylinder itself, while a genuine ancient document, is a piece of royal propaganda - a text designed to legitimize Cyrus's rule in Babylonian terms. It tells us what Cyrus wanted Babylonians to believe about him. It tells us rather less about the mechanics of his actual administration or the experience of ordinary people under his rule.

Historians differ on the degree to which Cyrus's reputation for tolerance and enlightened governance reflects genuine policy versus strategic self-presentation. The truth is probably that it was both - a ruler shrewd enough to understand that legitimacy was a resource, and that how you treated conquered peoples determined whether you would need to conquer them again.

What It Means

Leadership Style of Cyrus

What emerges from the evidence is a portrait of a leader who was, above all, adaptive. Cyrus did not impose a single template on every territory he absorbed. He read each situation differently - the Medes required integration, the Lydians required administration, the Babylonians required religious legitimacy, the Jewish captives required permission to go home. Each response was calibrated to the specific political and cultural conditions he encountered.

This flexibility was not weakness. It was a form of strategic intelligence that many conquerors of the ancient world lacked. Rulers who built empires through pure force often found those empires difficult to hold. Cyrus built an empire that lasted, in various forms, for more than two centuries after his death - until Alexander the Great finally dismantled it in 330 BCE.

His leadership also reveals a ruler who understood the difference between short-term military victory and long-term political stability. Winning a battle ends a war. Winning the loyalty - or at least the acquiescence - of a conquered population is what makes an empire governable.

Foundations of Empire-Building

Cyrus's methods established a template that would shape the Achaemenid Empire long after his death. His successors - Cambyses, Darius, Xerxes - inherited not just a territory but a governing philosophy: that a vast, multi-ethnic empire could be held together through a combination of central authority, regional autonomy, and the careful management of local religious and cultural identities.

This was genuinely new in the ancient world. Earlier empires had tended toward either direct domination - imposing the conqueror's culture and religion on the conquered - or loose tributary arrangements that provided little real integration. The Achaemenid model occupied a different space: a structured empire with real administrative coherence, but one that allowed considerable local variation within that structure.

That model would prove influential far beyond Persia. When Alexander the Great conquered the Persian Empire in 330 BCE, he did not simply destroy it. He studied it, adapted it, and in many ways continued it - adopting Persian administrative practices, wearing Persian dress, and presenting himself as a legitimate successor to Achaemenid kingship. The empire Cyrus built was so well-constructed that even its conqueror found it easier to inherit than to replace.

- In 553 BCE, Cyrus launched a rebellion against the Median dynasty that had long dominated Persia, and by 549 BCE he had founded the Achaemenid Persian Empire.

- Rather than destroying the Medes, Cyrus integrated them into his new empire - a pattern he would repeat with every major conquest.

- His 547 BCE campaign against Croesus of Lydia extended Persian power to the Aegean coast and brought enormous wealth into the empire.

- Cyrus's conquest of Babylon in 539 BCE was defined by political restraint: he honored Babylonian gods, preserved local institutions, and presented himself as a legitimate king rather than a foreign invader.

- His permission for Jewish captives to return to their homeland made him a celebrated figure in the Hebrew Bible - one of the few non-Israelite rulers described in terms of divine favor.

- Historians debate how much of Cyrus's reputation for tolerance reflects genuine policy versus deliberate royal propaganda, but the practical effects of his approach were real and lasting.

- His methods established the foundational logic of Achaemenid governance: central authority combined with regional flexibility and respect for local cultures.

- The empire he built lasted more than two centuries, and even Alexander the Great - who ultimately destroyed it - found Cyrus's administrative framework worth preserving.

Cyrus the Great did not simply conquer the ancient Near East. He reorganized it - and in doing so, he demonstrated something that rulers before and after him struggled to grasp: that the hardest part of building an empire is not taking territory, but making people willing to live within it. His legacy was not just the land he held, but the governing ideas he left behind. Those ideas would echo through Persian history, shape the ambitions of Alexander, and leave their traces in political thought that reached far beyond the ancient world.

Chapter 4
The War Against Wealth - Lydia

He was the richest man in the world, and he knew it. Croesus, King of Lydia, ruled from his gleaming capital at Sardis with a treasury so vast that his name became synonymous with fortune itself. We still use his name today - "rich as Croesus" - more than two and a half millennia after his kingdom turned to ash.

Wealth, it turns out, is not the same thing as wisdom. And an army built on gold is not necessarily an army that wins. In the middle of the sixth century BCE, Croesus commanded the richest kingdom the ancient world had ever seen, sat at the crossroads of civilizations, and chose to gamble it all on a war against a man who had nothing but speed, cunning, and an instinct for the kill. What followed was one of antiquity's starkest lessons in the difference between having everything and keeping it.

A King Who Redefined Riches

By the middle of the sixth century BCE, Lydia occupied a privileged position in the ancient world. Nestled in western Anatolia - what is now western Turkey - the kingdom sat at the crossroads of trade routes connecting the Aegean coast to the deeper interior of Asia. Its rivers reportedly ran with electrum, a natural alloy of gold and silver, and Lydia is widely credited as one of the first civilizations to mint standardized coinage. Money, in a very real sense, was a Lydian invention.

Croesus inherited this wealth and multiplied it. He extended Lydian dominance over the Greek city-states along the Ionian coast, extracting tribute while also cultivating a reputation as a generous patron of Greek culture. He sent lavish offerings to the Oracle at Delphi - golden lions, silver bowls, ingots of refined metal -

cementing his prestige across the Greek world. Greek writers would later describe his court as a place of almost mythological opulence.

But Croesus was not content to simply be rich. He was ambitious, and ambition in the ancient world had a way of colliding with geography. To his east, something new and dangerous was rising.

Croesus and the Rise of Cyrus

Cyrus the Great had, in the span of roughly a decade, transformed Persia from a regional kingdom into an empire of staggering reach. By the late 540s BCE, he had absorbed Media, subdued much of the Iranian plateau, and was pushing steadily westward. For Croesus, this was not merely a distant political development - it was a direct threat to Lydian power and, more personally, an affront to his own ambitions.

Croesus had also recently lost his brother-in-law Astyages, the Median king, to Cyrus's conquests. Revenge and strategy converged. He began to consider a preemptive strike against Persia before Cyrus could consolidate his western gains.

Before committing to war, however, Croesus did what any prudent ruler of the ancient world might do: he consulted the gods.

He sent emissaries to multiple oracles, reportedly testing their accuracy before trusting their counsel. The Oracle at Delphi, according to Greek tradition, passed his test. Croesus then posed the question that would define the rest of his life: if he crossed the Halys River and invaded Persia, what would happen?

The Oracle and Fatal Miscalculation

The Oracle's answer was famously, devastatingly ambiguous. If Croesus crossed the Halys and attacked Persia, the prophecy declared, he would destroy a great empire.

Croesus heard what he wanted to hear. A great empire would fall - surely his own, already mighty, would only grow greater. He returned to Sardis, gathered his forces, and prepared for war.

What the Oracle had not specified, of course, was *which* great empire would be destroyed.

This story comes to us primarily through Herodotus, the Greek historian writing roughly a century after the events themselves. Herodotus was a gifted storyteller with a keen eye for irony, and the tale of Croesus and the Oracle is one of his most celebrated passages. Historians today debate how literally to take it - whether the consultation happened exactly as described, whether the prophecy was recorded before or after the fact, or whether the story was shaped in retrospect to explain a catastrophic defeat. What seems clear is that Croesus did invade Persia, and that the decision proved fatal to his kingdom.

The deeper truth the story captures - that power and wealth can breed a dangerous overconfidence - rings as true now as it did in antiquity.

Battle of Pteria: The First Collision

In 547 or 546 BCE, Croesus led his forces across the Halys River into Cappadocia, the territory that marked the frontier between Lydia and the Persian sphere. Near the city of Pteria, the two armies met for the first time.

By most ancient accounts, the battle was inconclusive. Croesus commanded a formidable force - Lydian cavalry was renowned across the ancient world, and he had supplemented his own troops with Greek mercenaries and allied contingents. Cyrus, however, was no ordinary opponent. He had spent years fighting and winning against enemies far more experienced than Croesus, and he understood the importance of momentum.

The fighting at Pteria was fierce but produced no decisive result. Both sides suffered significant casualties. Croesus, finding himself unable to achieve a quick victory and aware that his forces had been bloodied, made a fateful decision: he would withdraw to Sardis for the winter, regroup, and return in the spring with a larger, reinforced army.

It was a reasonable calculation by the standards of ancient warfare, where campaigning seasons were real constraints. But Croesus had underestimated his opponent's willingness to ignore those conventions.

Cyrus did not go home. He followed.

Battle of Thymbra: The Camel Strategy

When Croesus learned that the Persian army was advancing directly on Sardis, he scrambled to assemble whatever forces he could muster. His Greek allies had not yet arrived. His reinforcements were still gathering. He rode out to meet Cyrus on the plain of Thymbra with what he had - and what he had was, above all, cavalry.

Lydian horsemen were the pride of the army, disciplined and battle-hardened. On open ground, they might have carried the day.

Cyrus, according to ancient sources, had anticipated exactly this. His solution was one of the more unusual tactical innovations recorded from the ancient world: he placed his baggage camels at the front of his formation, directly facing the Lydian cavalry.

Horses have a deep instinctive aversion to camels. The smell alone is enough to unsettle them. When the Lydian cavalry charged and the horses caught the scent of the camels, the animals panicked. Riders lost control. The charge collapsed into confusion before it ever made contact with the Persian line.

With the Lydian cavalry neutralized, Cyrus's infantry and his own horsemen swept through the disordered Lydian ranks. The battle turned into a rout. Croesus fled back to Sardis with the remnants of his army, and Cyrus pressed the pursuit without pause.

Herodotus recorded the camel tactic, and military historians have discussed it ever since. Whether it unfolded exactly as described remains debated, but the core outcome is not: Thymbra was a decisive Persian victory, and it effectively ended Lydian resistance in the field.

Fall of Sardis and Aftermath

Sardis, the Lydian capital, was considered nearly impregnable. Perched on a spur of Mount Tmolus, its citadel rose on cliffs that seemed to make direct assault impossible. Croesus retreated behind its walls and sent urgent appeals to his Greek and Egyptian allies, asking them to come to his aid within five months.

Cyrus did not give them five months.

He laid siege to the city and, according to Herodotus, his forces found a way in. A Persian soldier reportedly observed a Lydian defender descend the cliffs to retrieve a dropped helmet - revealing a path that the defenders had assumed no enemy would attempt. Persian troops scaled the cliffs along that route, and Sardis fell within fourteen days of the siege beginning.

Croesus was captured. His empire ceased to exist.

What happened to Croesus after his capture is one of the most debated questions in ancient history. Herodotus tells a dramatic story: Cyrus initially ordered Croesus burned alive on a pyre, but relented - moved either by the gods, by Croesus's philosophical composure, or by his own mercy - and spared him. In some versions of the tale, Croesus became a valued adviser at the Persian court. A Babylonian source, the Nabonidus Chronicle, makes no mention of Croesus's fate at all. Persian records are similarly silent on the details.

The honest answer is that we do not know with certainty what became of him. What we do know is that Lydia, its treasury, its trade networks, and its Ionian Greek subjects all passed into Persian hands. The conquest reshaped the balance of power across the eastern Mediterranean and set the stage for the conflicts between Persia and Greece that would define the following century.

What Historians Say

Greek Accounts vs. Reality

Herodotus is the primary source for almost everything we know about Croesus and the fall of Lydia, and that creates both opportunity and difficulty. He was writing roughly a century after the events, drawing on oral traditions, temple records, and the accounts of travelers and informants. His narrative is vivid and internally coherent, but it is also shaped by Greek literary conventions - particularly the theme of *hubris*, the overreach that brings down the mighty.

The Oracle story, the camel tactic, the pyre scene: all of these carry the hallmarks of moral fable as much as historical record. That does not mean they are false. It means they have been filtered through a tradition that valued instructive narrative alongside factual accuracy.

Archaeological evidence from Sardis confirms the city's destruction in the mid-sixth century BCE, broadly consistent with the ancient accounts. Persian administrative records confirm Cyrus's campaigns in western Anatolia. The broad outline - Croesus invaded, was defeated at Pteria and Thymbra, and lost Sardis - appears solid. The dramatic details surrounding the Oracle and the pyre are where historians exercise more caution.

The Fate of Croesus: An Unresolved Debate

Herodotus presents Croesus's survival as a near-miraculous intervention, with rain extinguishing the pyre at the last moment. Later Greek tradition expanded the story, depicting Croesus as a wise counselor who helped Cyrus avoid his own mistakes. These accounts are compelling, but they may reflect what Greek audiences *wanted* to believe - that wisdom could survive catastrophe, that a man of culture and refinement could find a place even in a conqueror's court.

The Nabonidus Chronicle, a Babylonian cuneiform document contemporary with the events, records Cyrus's campaigns but does not mention Croesus's fate. Some historians have suggested that Croesus may have been executed after all, and that the survival story was a later invention. Others argue that the silence of Babylonian records proves nothing, since they focused on different events and different regions.

The debate remains genuinely open. What is not in dispute is the political outcome: Lydia was gone, absorbed into the Persian Empire, and the world it had known would not return.

What It Means

Strategy vs. Wealth

Croesus's defeat offers one of history's clearest illustrations of the gap between economic power and military effectiveness. Lydia was, by any measure, the wealthier state. Its treasury funded a professional army, hired Greek mercenaries, and maintained alliances across the region. Croesus had every material advantage that money could buy.

Cyrus had something harder to purchase: strategic flexibility and the willingness to use it. He refused to observe the conventional pause in winter campaigning. He adapted his tactics to neutralize Lydia's greatest military asset. He moved faster than his opponent expected and struck before Croesus could consolidate his position.

Wealth can build armies. It cannot, by itself, make them win.

Lessons in Leadership and War

The story of Croesus also illustrates the dangers of confirmation bias - the human tendency to interpret ambiguous information in ways that confirm what we already want to believe. The Oracle's prophecy was genuinely unclear. Croesus chose the interpretation that flattered his ambitions and dismissed the possibility that it might mean something else entirely.

Leaders in every era have made the same mistake. They seek counsel, receive uncertain answers, and hear only the part that validates the course they had already decided to take.

Cyrus, by contrast, demonstrated the qualities that distinguished great commanders in the ancient world: adaptability, speed, and the ability to read an opponent's assumptions and turn them into vulnerabilities. He understood that Croesus's cavalry was his strength, and he neutralized it before the battle was decided.

The fall of Lydia was not simply a military event. It was a lesson in the limits of what money can protect, and in the kind of thinking - flexible, ruthless, creative - that tends to win when the two sides finally meet on the field.

- **Croesus** was the last king of Lydia, ruling in the sixth century BCE from the wealthy capital of Sardis; his name became a byword for extraordinary riches.

- **Lydia's wealth** came from its gold-bearing rivers and its role as a commercial crossroads; it is credited as one of the earliest civilizations to mint standardized coins.

- **Croesus consulted the Oracle at Delphi** before invading Persia; the prophecy that "a great empire would fall" was fatally misread as a promise of Lydian victory.

- **At the Battle of Pteria (547/6 BCE)**, the two armies fought to an inconclusive result; Croesus withdrew for winter, but Cyrus pursued immediately.

- **At the Battle of Thymbra**, Cyrus deployed camels against the Lydian cavalry, exploiting the horses' instinctive fear to neutralize Lydia's greatest military advantage.

- **Sardis fell within fourteen days** of the Persian siege; Croesus was captured and the Lydian Empire ceased to exist.

- **The fate of Croesus** - whether he was executed or spared to serve as a Persian adviser - remains historically unresolved, with Greek and Babylonian sources offering conflicting or silent testimony.

- **Cyrus's adaptability and speed** overcame Lydia's material superiority, demonstrating that wealth alone cannot substitute for military creativity and decisive action.

Croesus built the richest kingdom of his age and still lost everything in a single campaigning season. His story endured not because it was unusual but because it was, in some sense, universal - a warning about the seductive power of wealth to distort judgment and the danger of hearing only what we wish to hear. Cyrus, meanwhile, pressed on. With Lydia absorbed and the Ionian Greek cities now under Persian control, the empire's gaze turned westward - toward Egypt, toward the Aegean, and toward the long, complicated confrontation with Greece that would shape the ancient world for generations to come.

Chapter 5
The Silent Expansion East

An empire does not always announce itself with trumpets. Sometimes it moves quietly - through diplomacy, through settlement, through the slow absorption of peoples who never quite agreed to be absorbed.

The Achaemenid Persian Empire's expansion eastward into Central Asia remains one of the least-documented chapters in ancient imperial history. No single dramatic battle defines it. No famous speech commemorates it. Yet the territories the Persians came to control east of the Iranian plateau - the windswept plains of Bactria, the merchant corridors of Sogdia, the steppe frontiers where nomadic Sacae riders watched the horizon - were among the most strategically significant lands in the ancient world. Understanding how Persia came to hold them, and what holding them actually meant, requires reading between the lines of a history that left frustratingly few lines to begin with.

This chapter follows that eastward reach: the campaigns that pushed Persian authority into Central Asia, the distinct challenges posed by Bactria and Sogdia, the diplomatic calculations involved in managing the nomadic Sacae, and the gradual extension of Persian influence toward the Indus River. Along the way, it confronts an honest problem - the sources are thin, the archaeology is incomplete, and much of what we know comes filtered through later writers with their own agendas. What emerges is not a tidy story of conquest, but something more interesting: a picture of empire built as much through patience and strategy as through force.

Campaigns in Central Asia

Persia's move into Central Asia was not a single campaign but a process - one that unfolded across decades and likely involved a combination of military pressure, negotiated submission, and the gradual extension of administrative structures into territories that had never known centralized rule.

Beyond the eastern Iranian plateau's mountain ranges and desert margins lay a vast interior world. Central Asia was not empty. Settled agricultural communities worked the river valleys. Nomadic pastoralists ranged across the steppes. Trading peoples had long connected the resources of the east with the markets of the west. For a Persian king seeking to extend his reach, these territories offered both opportunity and complexity in equal measure.

Geography shaped these campaigns as much as political ambition did. Distances were enormous by ancient standards. Supply lines stretched thin. Terrain shifted from mountain passes to open steppe, each demanding different military approaches. Cavalry was essential. Logistics were everything. An army that could not feed itself in the field could not hold ground it had taken.

What the Persians appear to have understood - and what distinguished their eastern expansion from simple raiding - was that control required more than military victory. It required garrisons, local administrators, and the integration of conquered peoples into the imperial system in ways that made continued resistance more costly than cooperation.

Bactria and Sogdia

Of all the eastern territories, Bactria and Sogdia were the most consequential. Situated in what is today northern Afghanistan and the republics of Uzbekistan and Tajikistan, these regions sat at the crossroads of ancient trade routes connecting the Iranian world with India, China, and the steppe cultures of the north.

Bactria was defined by the Oxus River - the modern Amu Darya - and the fertile plains it watered. A land capable of supporting dense agricultural settlement, it had been incorporated into the Persian provincial system as a satrapy. Sogdia lay to its north, a region of oasis cities and merchant communities whose inhabitants would eventually become some of the ancient world's most accomplished long-distance traders.

Persian hold on these territories was real but always somewhat precarious. These were frontier lands, far from the imperial heartland at Persepolis or Susa, and the logistics of maintaining authority at such distances demanded constant attention. Local elites had to be cultivated. Tribute had to be collected without provoking rebellion. The balance between imperial extraction and local autonomy was a permanent negotiation.

Later history offers a sharp illustration of just how contested these territories were. When Alexander the Great swept into Bactria and Sogdiana in the 320s BCE, he encountered some of the fiercest resistance of his entire campaign - resistance that required years of brutal counterinsurgency warfare to suppress. That Alexander, one of history's most formidable military commanders, found these regions so difficult to pacify tells us something important about the character of Persian rule there. It was authority maintained through ongoing effort, not passive acceptance.

Alexander's eventual colonization of Bactria and Sogdiana - establishing Greek settlements and installing Macedonian administrators - dramatically altered the region's cultural dynamics. But that transformation only became possible because the Persian imperial framework had already integrated these territories into a broader administrative world. Alexander, in many ways, inherited a structure and then reshaped it.

The Sacae and Diplomatic Strategy

Beyond the settled lands of Bactria and Sogdia lay the steppe - and the steppe belonged to the Sacae.

The Sacae were a loosely affiliated grouping of nomadic and semi-nomadic peoples who ranged across the vast grasslands north and east of the settled Persian provinces. Skilled horsemen and formidable fighters, they were deeply resistant to the kind of territorial control that empires preferred. They did not build cities that could be captured or hold fixed positions that could be besieged. They moved.

For the Persians, the Sacae represented a strategic challenge that conventional military means alone could not solve. A campaign against nomadic peoples on open steppe risked becoming an exhausting pursuit with no decisive endpoint. The Persians appear to have recognized this, and their approach reflected a more sophisticated calculus - one that blended military demonstration with diplomatic engagement.

Incorporating steppe peoples into the imperial system meant offering something in return for cooperation: recognition, trade access, gifts, and the prestige that came from formal association with a great empire. Some Sacae groups appear to have provided military contingents to Persian armies, suggesting a relationship of negotiated alliance rather than simple subjugation. Others remained outside Persian control entirely, a permanent reminder that the empire's eastern frontier was a zone of influence rather than a hard boundary.

This diplomatic flexibility was not weakness. It was pragmatism. An empire that exhausted itself fighting every frontier people it encountered would have little energy left to govern the territories it already held. Managing the Sacae through a combination of deterrence and engagement was, in strategic terms, a rational choice - one that kept the eastern frontier stable enough to allow Persian attention to focus elsewhere.

Expansion Toward the Indus

The easternmost reach of Persian imperial ambition pointed toward the Indus River and the subcontinent beyond. By the reign of Darius

I in the late sixth century BCE, Persian authority had extended into the northwestern regions of the Indian subcontinent - territories corresponding roughly to parts of modern Pakistan and Afghanistan.

This expansion brought Persia into contact with a world shaped by the long legacy of the Indus Valley Civilization, whose urban centers had declined around 1800 BCE, likely influenced by shifts in river systems. What remained was a patchwork of successor cultures and communities that the Persians now encountered as they pushed their administrative reach toward the Indus.

The region became a Persian satrapy, contributing tribute and, notably, soldiers to Persian armies. Indian contingents are recorded among the forces that Xerxes led westward during his invasion of Greece - a remarkable illustration of just how far the Persian imperial network extended. A soldier from the Indus valley fighting on the plains of Greece: the ancient world was more connected than it is sometimes given credit for.

Control of the Indus region also gave Persia access to riverine trade routes and the broader commercial networks that linked the subcontinent with the Persian Gulf and the Iranian plateau. Empire, at its most functional, was always partly an economic enterprise.

What Historians Say

Limited Sources and Archaeology

Reconstructing the Persian expansion into Central Asia is genuinely difficult work. Ancient sources for this period are sparse, often fragmentary, and frequently written by Greek authors whose interest in Persian Central Asia was incidental to other concerns. Persian administrative records, where they survive, tend toward the practical: tribute lists, ration accounts, logistical documents. They confirm that these territories existed within the imperial system but rarely explain how they came to be there.

Archaeology offers some help, but Central Asia's archaeological record for this period remains incompletely excavated and unevenly published. Political instability across the twentieth century complicated sustained fieldwork, and much of what lies beneath the soil of Bactria and Sogdia has yet to be systematically studied.

One striking illustration of how much remains unknown: the Kushans, who came to dominate Central Asia between roughly 200 BCE and 700 CE, used a writing system that scholars have still not fully deciphered. If a later empire's script remains partially opaque, the documentary traces of Persian administration in the same region are even harder to recover.

What We Can Infer

Despite these limitations, historians can draw reasonable inferences from what survives. The inclusion of eastern territories in Persian tribute lists confirms their administrative integration. Resistance Alexander encountered in Bactria and Sogdia suggests that Persian authority there, while real, had never fully suppressed local political identity. Indian soldiers serving in Persian armies confirms that the Indus satrapy was genuinely incorporated into imperial military structures.

Scholars generally agree that Persian expansion into Central Asia was a process of layered control - military where necessary, diplomatic where possible, administrative throughout - rather than a single dramatic conquest. The empire's eastern frontier was always a negotiated space.

What It Means

Expansion Through Strategy

The Persian expansion eastward offers a case study in how ancient empires actually worked - not as monolithic machines of conquest, but as adaptive systems that combined force, diplomacy, and administration in shifting proportions depending on local conditions.

In Bactria and Sogdia, where settled populations and existing political structures provided something to work with, Persian administration could take root in recognizable form. On the steppe, where the Sacae defied territorial logic, the empire had to operate differently - projecting power through alliance and deterrence rather than occupation. Near the Indus, where ancient urban traditions had faded but commercial networks persisted, Persian control plugged into existing economic flows.

None of this was inevitable. It required constant management, constant recalibration. The "silent" quality of this expansion - its relative absence from dramatic historical narratives - reflects not insignificance but a different kind of imperial work: the unglamorous labor of maintaining authority across vast distances and diverse peoples.

Securing Trade and Stability

What the eastern expansion ultimately secured was something the ancient world valued enormously: connectivity. The territories Persia controlled in Central Asia sat astride the routes that would later be formalized as the Silk Road. Goods, ideas, and people moved through Bactria and Sogdia long before any empire claimed them, and Persian control of these corridors gave the empire both economic benefit and strategic depth.

Stability on the eastern frontier also freed Persian military and administrative attention for other theaters - the western frontier with Greece, the management of Egypt, the internal politics of the imperial court. An empire that could not secure its rear could not project power forward. In this sense, the quiet work of eastern expansion was foundational to everything else the Achaemenid Empire attempted.

Quick Summary

- Persian expansion into Central Asia was a gradual process combining military campaigns, diplomatic engagement, and administrative integration - not a single conquest.

- Bactria and Sogdia were key eastern satrapies, sitting at the crossroads of trade routes connecting Persia with India, the steppe, and eventually China.

- Fierce resistance Alexander the Great encountered in these regions after 330 BCE suggests Persian authority there was real but always contested.

- The Sacae, nomadic peoples of the steppe, were managed through a combination of military deterrence and diplomatic negotiation rather than direct territorial control.

- Persian expansion toward the Indus brought the subcontinent's northwestern regions into the imperial system, with Indian soldiers eventually serving in Persian armies as far away as Greece.

- Ancient sources for this period are sparse and often filtered through Greek perspectives; archaeology in Central Asia remains incomplete, leaving significant gaps in our understanding.

- The eastern expansion secured trade corridor access and frontier stability that underpinned the broader Achaemenid imperial project.

The Persian reach into Central Asia left no single monument to mark its achievement - no triumphal arch, no famous battlefield. What it left instead was a framework: an administrative and diplomatic architecture that shaped how later empires, from Alexander's successors to the Kushans, would approach the same territories. Empires that followed often built on Persian foundations without

acknowledging them. That, perhaps, is the quietest kind of legacy -
and in its own way, the most durable.

Chapter 6
The Fall of Babylon

On the night of October 12, 539 BCE, Persian soldiers walked through the gates of the greatest city on earth - and almost no one tried to stop them.

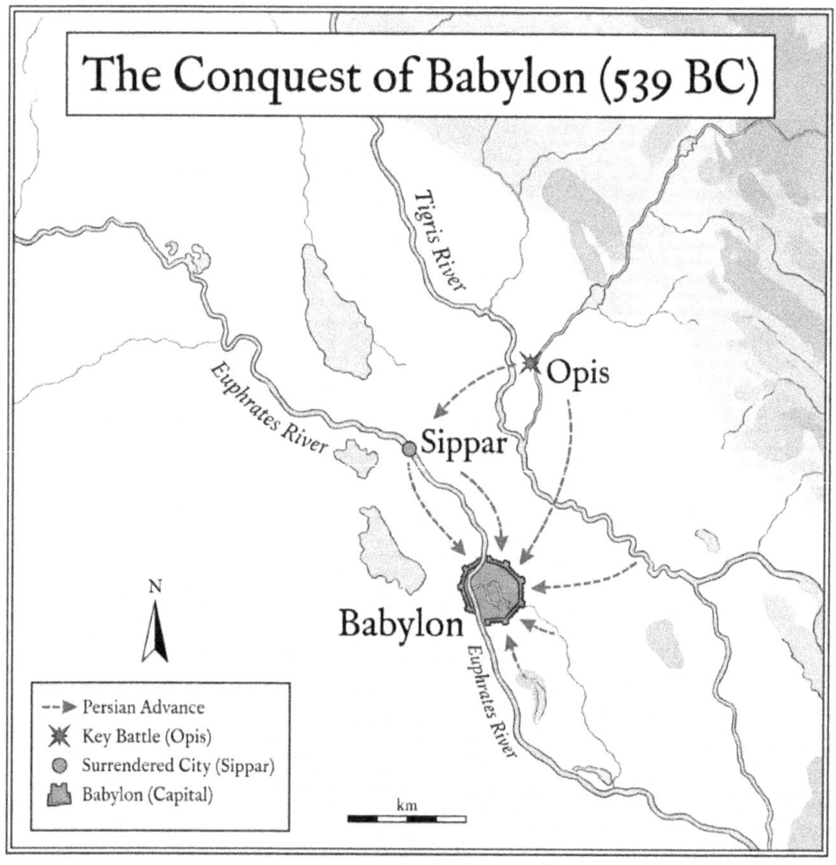

Babylon Campaign Map

Babylon was not some provincial outpost ripe for the taking. It was the beating heart of an empire that had endured for centuries, a city of towering walls, sacred temples, and a population that numbered in the hundreds of thousands. Yet it fell without a siege, without a prolonged battle, without the kind of catastrophic destruction that had leveled cities from Nineveh to Jerusalem in the decades before. When Cyrus the Great entered Babylon on October 29, 539 BCE - seventeen days after his army - he did so not as a destroyer but, at least according to the story he told the world, as a liberator.

How does the mightiest city of the ancient world fall so quietly? The answer lies in a combination of internal collapse, political miscalculation, and one of history's most effective propaganda campaigns. Babylon did not simply lose a battle. It lost faith in its own king - and Cyrus was shrewd enough to exploit that loss completely.

Babylon Under Nabonidus

To understand why Babylon fell the way it did, you have to understand the man who was supposed to defend it.

Nabonidus was the last king of the Neo-Babylonian Empire, and by most accounts, a deeply unusual ruler. He came to power around 556 BCE, not through dynastic succession in the traditional sense, but through a path that left questions about his legitimacy from the start. Where his predecessors - including the famous Nebuchadnezzar II - had ruled as warrior-kings deeply embedded in Babylonian religious life, Nabonidus seemed almost allergic to the role.

His most consequential decision was to leave. For roughly a decade, Nabonidus abandoned Babylon and relocated to Tayma, an oasis city deep in the Arabian desert. Historians have debated his reasons - trade routes, personal religious interests, political exile - but the effect was the same regardless of the cause. Babylon, the empire's capital and spiritual center, was left without its king.

This mattered enormously. Babylonian kingship was not merely political. It was religious. Every year, the king was required to participate in the Akitu festival, the sacred New Year ceremony in which he symbolically renewed his covenant with Marduk, the chief god of Babylon. Without the king's presence, the festival could not be properly performed. Without the festival, the divine order that legitimized Babylonian rule was left suspended, year after year.

Nabonidus left his son Belshazzar in charge of day-to-day administration, but a regent is not a king. The city's priests, merchants, and citizens watched the years pass without their ruler, without the sacred rites, without the symbolic renewal that held the empire together.

Political and Religious Tension

By the time Cyrus was marching westward, Babylon was already fraying from within.

Nabonidus had compounded his absence with a religious policy that alienated the most powerful institution in the city: the priesthood of Marduk. He elevated the moon god Sin above Marduk in the imperial religious hierarchy - a move that struck the Babylonian clergy as not just unorthodox but offensive.

The priests of Marduk were not simply spiritual figures. They controlled vast temple estates, managed significant economic resources, and wielded enormous influence over public opinion. Losing their support was not a minor inconvenience. It was a structural crack in the foundation of the empire.

Nabonidus eventually returned to Babylon as the Persian threat became impossible to ignore, but the damage was done. He had spent years away from his capital, neglected the religious duties that defined legitimate kingship, and antagonized the very institutions that might have rallied the population to resist an invader.

Meanwhile, Cyrus had spent years building exactly the opposite reputation. After defeating the Median king Astyages around 550 BCE and conquering Lydia around 547 BCE, he had developed a consistent pattern: take cities with minimal destruction, respect local customs, and present himself as a restorer of order rather than a conqueror. Word traveled. Reputations, in the ancient world, were a form of military power.

By 539 BCE, the contrast could not have been sharper. On one side, an absent king who had insulted his gods and ignored his people. On the other, a conqueror who promised to do neither.

The Battle of Opis

The campaign itself began with blood.

Before Babylon could fall quietly, Cyrus had to break Babylonian military resistance in the field. That confrontation came at Opis, a city on the Tigris River north of Babylon. The battle was a decisive Persian victory, and its aftermath was brutal - ancient sources indicate that Cyrus ordered a massacre of the Babylonian forces there.

Opis mattered strategically and psychologically. It shattered whatever organized military resistance Nabonidus could mount and sent a clear message to the cities between the battlefield and Babylon itself: the Persian army had arrived, it had won, and resistance would be costly.

Nabonidus, by this point, was attempting to manage a crisis he had spent years creating. His forces had been broken in the open field. His allies were limited. His standing with the Babylonian priesthood and population had been eroded by years of neglect and religious controversy. He was, in every meaningful sense, isolated.

What followed suggests that the psychological blow of Opis was as significant as the military one. Cities that might have held out began to calculate their options - and for many, surrender looked considerably more appealing than the alternative.

The Fall of Sippar and Entry into Babylon

Sippar, a major Babylonian city north of the capital, fell to Persian forces without resistance. The ease of its capture signaled what was coming.

On October 12, 539 BCE, Persian forces entered Babylon itself. The Nabonidus Chronicle - a Babylonian administrative document recording the events of the period - describes the entry in strikingly understated terms. No great siege. No burning of temples. No mass slaughter of civilians. The Persian army moved into the city, and Babylon, for all its legendary walls and storied history, simply changed hands.

Nabonidus was captured. The exact circumstances of his fate remain unclear from the sources available, but he did not die in battle defending his capital. He was taken prisoner - a final, inglorious end to a reign defined by absence and miscalculation.

Cyrus himself entered the city on October 29, seventeen days after his army. The delay was almost certainly deliberate. His generals had secured the city; Cyrus's entrance was a carefully staged event, not a military necessity. He came not as a soldier but as a king - and, crucially, as a worshipper of Marduk.

Cyrus as Liberator

What happened next was as much theater as governance - and it worked.

Cyrus presented himself to the Babylonians not as a foreign conqueror but as the chosen instrument of Marduk himself. The god, the story went, had grown disgusted with Nabonidus's neglect and impiety, and had reached out across the world to find a worthy king. He had chosen Cyrus. The Persian king had come not to destroy Babylon but to restore it.

This narrative was not subtle. But it did not need to be. It spoke directly to the grievances that had accumulated under Nabonidus - the abandoned festivals, the demotion of Marduk, the years of absence. Cyrus offered the priests of Marduk exactly what they had been denied: a king who would perform the proper rites, restore the proper order, and treat their god with the respect he deserved.

He also made practical gestures to match the rhetoric. Peoples who had been displaced or deported under Babylonian rule - including, according to biblical accounts, Jewish exiles - were permitted to return to their homelands. Local customs and religious practices were respected rather than suppressed. The administrative machinery of Babylon was largely kept intact, with Persian oversight layered on top rather than replacing it wholesale.

Whether Cyrus genuinely believed any of this, or whether it was pure political calculation, is a question history cannot fully answer. What is clear is that it was extraordinarily effective.

What Historians Say

The Cyrus Cylinder

Our most famous source for the fall of Babylon is a small clay cylinder discovered in the ruins of the city in 1879. Written in Babylonian cuneiform, the Cyrus Cylinder presents the conquest from Cyrus's own perspective - or rather, from the perspective of the scribes he employed to shape his image.

The cylinder describes Marduk surveying the world and selecting Cyrus as the righteous king who would end Nabonidus's misrule. It portrays Cyrus entering Babylon peacefully, to the joy of its inhabitants, and restoring the gods and peoples that Nabonidus had displaced. It is, in short, a masterpiece of ancient public relations.

Historians treat it with appropriate caution. The cylinder is propaganda - produced by the victor, designed to legitimize conquest by recasting it as divine rescue. But propaganda is not the same as pure fiction. The cylinder's claims about peaceful entry, respect for local religion, and the repatriation of displaced peoples are broadly consistent with other sources, including the Nabonidus Chronicle. The spin is real; so, it seems, are many of the underlying facts.

Some scholars have pointed to the cylinder as an early articulation of something resembling religious tolerance and human rights - a reading that has proven controversial. The cylinder was not a universal declaration. It was a political document aimed at a specific audience, making specific promises to consolidate specific power. Reading it as a timeless charter of liberty says more about modern hopes than ancient intentions.

The Nabonidus Chronicle

Where the Cyrus Cylinder tells us what Cyrus wanted the world to believe, the Nabonidus Chronicle offers something closer to a contemporary administrative record. This Babylonian document covers the final years of Nabonidus's reign and records the Persian conquest with a matter-of-fact brevity that is, in its own way, more striking than any triumphalist inscription.

The chronicle confirms the fall of Sippar, the entry of Persian forces into Babylon, and the capture of Nabonidus. Its tone is not celebratory, but neither is it a lament. It reads like a ledger entry - as if the scribes recording it had simply accepted that one era had ended and another had begun.

That tone tells its own story. A population genuinely shocked or traumatized by a violent conquest would likely have produced different records. The chronicle's relative calm suggests that for many Babylonians, the transition - whatever its costs - was not experienced as catastrophe.

What It Means

Why the Conquest Was Bloodless

Babylon's fall without a major siege was not a miracle of Persian military genius. It was the predictable outcome of a kingdom that had spent years undermining its own foundations.

Nabonidus had alienated the priesthood, neglected the capital, failed to perform the religious duties that legitimized his rule, and left his military exposed at Opis. By the time Cyrus arrived, the social contract between king and city had already broken down. There was no unified will to resist - not among the priests, not among the merchants, not, it seems, among much of the population.

Cyrus understood this. His campaign against Babylon was as much diplomatic as military. He cultivated the support of the Marduk priesthood before his army ever reached the city walls. He positioned himself as the solution to a problem the Babylonians had been living with for years. When his forces arrived, many within the city likely saw them not as invaders but as the answer to a prayer - quite literally, if you accepted the Marduk narrative.

Propaganda vs. Reality

The image of Cyrus as a benevolent liberator has proven remarkably durable - durable enough that it has sometimes been accepted too uncritically.

Cyrus was a conqueror. He built an empire through military force, and the campaign that ended at Babylon began with a massacre at Opis. His tolerance for local customs and religions was genuine in many respects, but it was also strategically useful: a conquered population that feels respected is cheaper to govern than one in permanent revolt. Enlightened self-interest and genuine magnanimity are not mutually exclusive, but they are not the same thing either.

The Cyrus Cylinder, whatever its propagandistic intent, does reflect a real approach to imperial governance - one that stood in contrast to the more brutal methods of some Assyrian predecessors. That contrast was meaningful to the people who lived through it. But the Persian Empire was still an empire, built on conquest and maintained by power. The story of Babylon's fall is a story about how empires are won - and how the winners write the history that follows.

- **Nabonidus**, the last Neo-Babylonian king, weakened his empire by abandoning Babylon for roughly a decade, neglecting the sacred Akitu festival, and alienating the powerful priesthood of Marduk.

- **Cyrus the Great** had already built a reputation for respecting local customs and religions after conquering the Medes around 550 BCE and Lydia around 547 BCE.

- **The Battle of Opis** broke Babylonian military resistance before the capital itself was threatened, paving the way for swift collapse.

- **Sippar fell without resistance**, and on **October 12, 539 BCE**, Persian forces entered Babylon; Cyrus himself followed on **October 29**.

- Cyrus presented himself as the chosen of Marduk, restoring the religious order Nabonidus had disrupted - a narrative that resonated deeply with Babylon's priests and people.

- **The Cyrus Cylinder** is the primary source for Cyrus's self-presentation; historians read it as sophisticated propaganda that nonetheless reflects real policies of religious tolerance and repatriation.

- **The Nabonidus Chronicle**, a Babylonian administrative record, corroborates the peaceful entry and the capture of Nabonidus with striking matter-of-factness.

- Babylon's bloodless fall resulted less from Persian mercy than from years of internal decay - a kingdom that had already lost faith in its own king.

The fall of Babylon did not end civilization - it redirected it. Under Persian rule, the city continued to function as a major administrative and cultural center, its temples intact, its traditions preserved. But the Neo-Babylonian Empire was finished, and with it the last great

Mesopotamian dynasty that had dominated the ancient Near East for generations. What replaced it was something new: a Persian Empire stretching from the Mediterranean to the Indus Valley, governed by a king who had learned that the most durable conquests are the ones that make the conquered feel, at least for a while, that they have been saved.

Chapter 7
The King Who Did Not Destroy

The Cyrus Cylinder

When Cyrus the Great rode into Babylon in 539 BCE, the city did not burn. No temples were looted. No gods were smashed. For a conqueror in the ancient world, this was almost unthinkable.

Most empires of the ancient Near East announced their power through destruction - toppled statues, deported populations, gods carried off as trophies to the victor's capital. Cyrus did something different. He walked into one of the greatest cities on earth and told its people, in effect, that nothing would change. Their gods would remain. Their priests would keep their positions. Their rituals would continue undisturbed. And for the peoples who had been dragged to Babylon as captives - among them the Jewish exiles from Jerusalem - he went further still. He told them they could go home.

What Cyrus actually did when he took Babylon, how he treated the peoples under his rule, and why his approach - whether driven by genuine conviction or cold political calculation - helped build one of the most durable empires the ancient world had ever seen: these are questions that still matter, three millennia later.

A Conqueror Who Called Himself a Liberator

Entering Babylon

By 539 BCE, Cyrus had already assembled the largest empire the world had yet known. He had swept through Media, Lydia, and the Iranian plateau, absorbing kingdoms with a speed that left his contemporaries struggling to explain it. Babylon, the jewel of Mesopotamia, was his final great prize in the west.

Babylon fell without the kind of catastrophic siege that had defined so many ancient conquests. Ancient sources suggest the city capitulated with relatively little resistance, and Cyrus entered not as a destroyer but as a restorer - at least, that is how he chose to present himself. He made offerings to Marduk, the chief god of Babylon, and declared himself the god's chosen servant. He did not impose Persian religion. He did not dismantle the Babylonian priesthood. He positioned himself, with considerable care, as the legitimate continuation of Babylonian kingship rather than its termination.

This was a declaration as much as a conquest. Cyrus was telling the Babylonians - and anyone else paying attention - that his empire was not built on ruin.

The Politics of Piety

Religious Policies Across the Empire

What Cyrus practiced in Babylon was not an isolated gesture. Across the territories he controlled, he adopted a consistent approach: local religions would be respected, local customs preserved, and local elites kept in place where they could be useful. Persian governors administered the empire, but they did so within a framework that allowed conquered peoples to maintain their identities.

This stood in deliberate contrast to the methods of the Assyrians, who had made deportation and cultural suppression into instruments of imperial policy. Cyrus had studied what worked and what didn't. Forced assimilation created resentment. Resentment created rebellion. Rebellion was expensive.

His approach was not passive tolerance in the modern sense. It was active, calculated accommodation. By honoring local gods, Cyrus gained the loyalty of local priests, who were often among the most influential figures in ancient societies. By preserving temples, he preserved the institutions that organized community life. By allowing exiled peoples to return home, he transformed potential enemies into grateful subjects.

"Let My People Go" - The Jewish Exiles

The Decree and the Return

Among the most consequential acts of Cyrus's reign was his treatment of the Jewish exiles in Babylon. Since the Babylonian king Nebuchadnezzar II had destroyed Jerusalem and its Temple in 586

BCE, a significant portion of the Jewish population had lived in exile - displaced from their homeland, their Temple in ruins, their religious life fundamentally disrupted.

Cyrus changed this. According to the Book of Ezra, he issued a decree permitting the Jewish exiles to return to Jerusalem and rebuild their Temple. The text frames Cyrus in explicitly theological terms - as an instrument of the God of Israel, charged with restoring the Jerusalem Temple. "The Lord, the God of heaven, has given me all the kingdoms of the earth," the decree begins, "and he has appointed me to build a temple for him at Jerusalem."

Whether Cyrus actually used those words is a matter historians debate. What is not in doubt is that he issued some form of authorization for the exiles' return and for the Temple's reconstruction. Jewish communities began making their way back to Judah. The rebuilding of what would become the Second Temple was set in motion.

For Jewish history, this moment was transformative. Cyrus appears in the Hebrew Bible not as a foreign king but as a figure of divine purpose - even as a messiah, one of the very few non-Israelites to receive that designation in the biblical text.

Restoring What Others Had Broken

The Return of Gods and Sacred Objects

Cyrus's policy extended beyond people. He also ordered the return of sacred objects that the Babylonians had confiscated from conquered peoples - cult statues, temple vessels, religious artifacts brought to Babylon as symbols of domination. Returning them reversed that symbolism. It said, in the clearest possible terms, that the old order of conquest and humiliation was over.

For the Jewish exiles, this meant the return of the sacred vessels Nebuchadnezzar had taken from the Jerusalem Temple. For other peoples across the region, it meant the restoration of gods to their proper sanctuaries. Temples that had fallen into disrepair under Babylonian neglect were to be rebuilt and re-staffed.

This was an enormous undertaking, requiring financial support, administrative coordination, and political will. That Cyrus committed to it suggests the policy was not merely rhetorical. He was investing in the goodwill of his subjects in a very concrete way.

What the Evidence Actually Says

Biblical Accounts and Archaeological Reality

Two primary sources illuminate Cyrus's policies: the biblical texts, particularly the books of Ezra and Isaiah, and the Cyrus Cylinder, a clay barrel inscription discovered in Babylon in 1879. Each tells a version of the same story, and each requires careful reading.

The biblical account is unambiguous in its admiration. Isaiah, written before Cyrus's rise, appears to prophesy his arrival as a deliverer. Ezra records his decree in terms that present him as an agent of divine will. These texts were written by people who had every reason to view Cyrus favorably - he had, after all, ended their exile.

The Cyrus Cylinder offers a different angle. Written in Akkadian, the language of Babylon, it presents Cyrus as the chosen servant of Marduk, who had grown displeased with the previous Babylonian king Nabonidus. Cyrus, the cylinder claims, was invited into Babylon by Marduk himself to restore proper worship and return displaced peoples to their homelands.

Historians recognize both texts as propagandistic in nature. Neither is a neutral account. The cylinder was produced by Cyrus's own court to legitimize his rule in Babylonian terms; the biblical texts reflect the perspective of a community that owed its restoration to his policies. What both sources share, however, is the same core narrative: Cyrus as liberator, restorer, and divinely sanctioned ruler. That both Persian and Jewish traditions converged on this image suggests it was not entirely invented.

Reading the Cylinder Carefully

The Cyrus Cylinder has sometimes been called the world's first human rights document - a claim that modern scholars treat with considerable skepticism. The cylinder is not a universal declaration of liberty. It is a piece of royal propaganda, carefully crafted to appeal to Babylonian religious sensibilities and justify Persian rule. Its language of liberation is real, but its purpose is legitimacy.

That said, propaganda only works when it reflects something people are willing to believe. The cylinder's claims about Cyrus's benevolence had to be at least partially credible to function. The policies it describes - returning exiles, restoring temples, respecting local gods - appear to have been real, not just rhetorical flourishes.

Tolerance or Strategy? The Honest Answer Is Both

Why Cyrus Governed the Way He Did

Modern readers sometimes want Cyrus to be a visionary of religious freedom - a proto-liberal in a world of tyrants. That reading is too simple. Cyrus was a conqueror and an empire-builder, and his policies served his empire's interests with remarkable effectiveness.

Allowing peoples to maintain their religions and customs was cheaper than suppressing them. It reduced the administrative burden of governing vast, diverse territories. It turned potential rebels into cooperative subjects. It gave local elites - priests, administrators, landowners - a stake in the stability of Persian rule. Every temple Cyrus restored was, in a sense, an investment in loyalty.

But strategy and genuine policy preference are not mutually exclusive. Cyrus may well have believed that this approach was simply right - that conquered peoples deserved to keep their gods and their ways of life. The ancient world was not without rulers who held such views. What made Cyrus exceptional was not that he thought this way, but that he had the power and the consistency to act on it across an empire stretching from the Aegean to the borders of India.

The Stability That Followed

The results spoke for themselves. The Achaemenid Empire that Cyrus founded endured for more than two centuries - an extraordinary run in a region where empires rose and collapsed with regularity. His successors, Cambyses and Darius, inherited a political structure built on accommodation rather than coercion, and while they did not always maintain his standards, the framework held.

Peoples who felt their identities were respected had less reason to revolt. Communities allowed to rebuild their temples had something to protect. The Jewish community that returned to Jerusalem under Cyrus's decree became, in time, a stable and productive part of the Persian imperial world. None of this was accidental. It was the long-term dividend of a policy that treated subjects as participants rather than possessions.

- Cyrus the Great conquered Babylon in 539 BCE without destroying the city or its religious institutions, presenting himself as a liberator rather than a conqueror.

- His religious policies allowed conquered peoples to maintain their own gods, customs, and temples - a deliberate departure from Assyrian-style suppression.

- He issued a decree permitting Jewish exiles to return to Jerusalem and rebuild the Temple, an act recorded in the Book of Ezra and celebrated in Jewish tradition.

- Cyrus ordered the return of sacred objects taken by the Babylonians, restoring them to their original temples across the region.

- The Cyrus Cylinder, discovered in 1879, presents his rule in Babylonian religious terms - as the fulfillment of Marduk's will - and is best understood as sophisticated royal propaganda rather than a universal rights declaration.

- Both biblical and archaeological sources reflect Persian efforts to legitimize Cyrus's rule through narratives of divine sanction and liberation.

- His tolerant policies were almost certainly strategic as well as principled, but the two motivations reinforced each other, producing an empire of remarkable stability and longevity.

Cyrus the Great did not invent the idea of treating conquered peoples with a degree of dignity - earlier rulers had experimented with similar approaches. What he did was practice it systematically, at scale, across one of the largest empires the ancient world had ever seen. The empire he built outlasted him by nearly two centuries, and the memory of what he did outlasted the empire itself. Across three millennia, his name appears in Jewish scripture, Persian legend, and Greek history alike - always as something more than just a conqueror.

What comes next in the story of the ancient Near East would be shaped, in no small part, by the world he made possible.

Chapter 8
How Cyrus Ruled the World

At its height, the Achaemenid Empire stretched from the Aegean coast of modern Turkey to the edges of Central Asia - a landmass so vast that no single army, no single road, and no single king could hold it together by force alone. Cyrus the Great understood this. And so he built something more durable than walls.

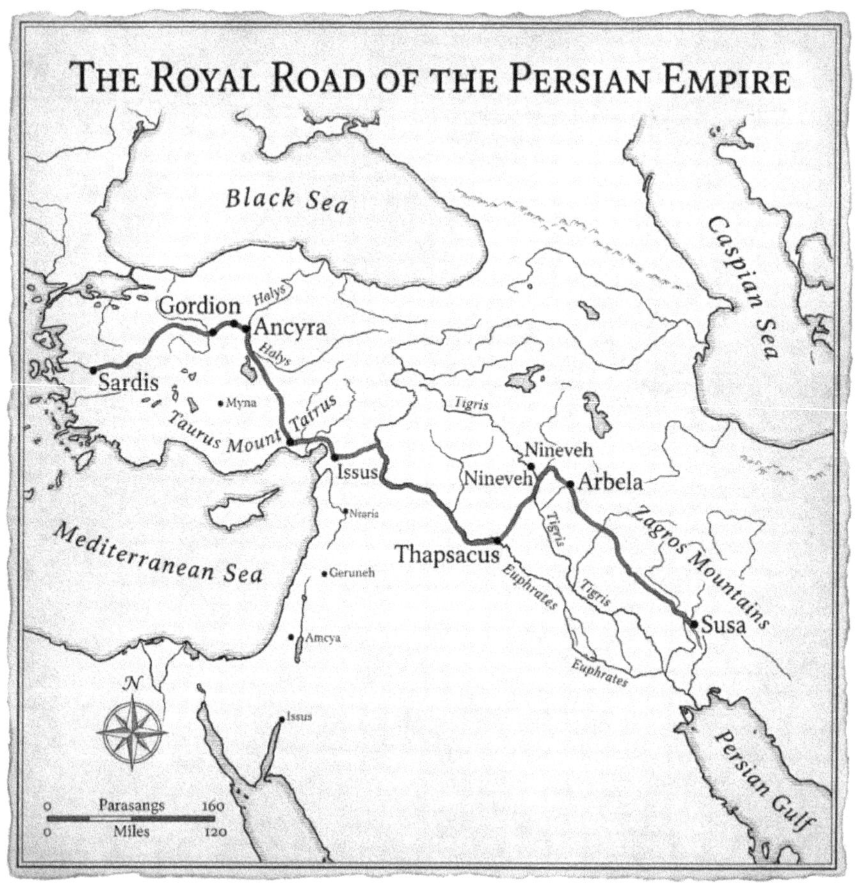

Royal Road Map

What Cyrus created between 576 and 530 BCE was not merely an empire in the military sense - it was a system. A framework of governance so elegantly designed that it would outlast him by two centuries, influence the administrative logic of Alexander the Great, and echo in the bureaucratic structures of empires that came long after. The Persian model of rule was, in many ways, the first serious answer to one of history's most persistent questions: how do you govern people who are nothing like you?

What follows is the architecture of that answer - the provincial governors who kept order across thousands of miles, the road that stitched the empire together, the economic networks that made it profitable, and the capital city that announced Persian ambition to the ancient world.

The Satrapy System: Governing Without Micromanaging

The first problem of empire is distance. A king in his palace cannot personally settle a dispute in a village three months' journey away. He cannot collect taxes, raise soldiers, or maintain order in a province he has never visited. Every ancient empire grappled with this problem. Most solved it badly.

Cyrus solved it with satraps.

A satrap - from the Old Persian *xšaθrapāvan*, meaning "protector of the kingdom" - was a regional governor appointed to administer one of the empire's provinces, known as satrapies. These were not mere local chieftains or puppet rulers. Satraps held genuine authority: they collected taxes, administered justice, commanded local military forces, and maintained the peace within their territories. They were, in effect, the empire's hands in places where the king's eyes could not easily reach.

What made the system work was its balance of delegation and accountability. Satraps were powerful, but they were not unchecked.

The king retained the right to appoint and dismiss them. Royal inspectors - sometimes called the "eyes and ears of the king" - traveled throughout the satrapies to audit their conduct and report back to the center. Local authority paired with central oversight gave the empire flexibility without sacrificing coherence.

The genius of the arrangement was also cultural. Rather than imposing a single Persian identity on conquered peoples, Cyrus allowed satrapies to retain their own languages, customs, and local traditions, provided they paid their taxes and kept the peace. A Babylonian satrap might govern in ways that looked distinctly Babylonian. A Lydian province might maintain its own religious practices. The empire did not demand uniformity - it demanded loyalty, and it was willing to be flexible about everything else.

This tolerance was not idealism. It was strategy. An empire that crushes local identity invites constant rebellion. One that accommodates it can redirect local energy into imperial service.

The Royal Road: Speed as a Tool of Power

An empire that cannot communicate is an empire that cannot respond. News of a revolt, a drought, a border incursion - any of these required the king to act quickly, and quickly meant getting information from the periphery to the center before the situation deteriorated beyond control.

Cyrus's answer was infrastructure. Under his reign, the Persians developed an extensive road network, the most celebrated stretch of which became known as the Royal Road. Running roughly from Sardis on the Aegean coast to Susa in the heart of Persia, this route connected the western edge of the empire to its administrative core across a distance of some 2,700 kilometers.

What made the Royal Road remarkable was not just its length but its speed. A system of relay stations - positioned at regular intervals along the route - allowed royal couriers to pass messages from station to station without stopping. Fresh horses waited at each post. Riders changed mounts, handed off their dispatches, and the message continued without pause, day and night. By some ancient accounts, a message could travel the full length of the road in a matter of days - a journey that would take an ordinary traveler months on foot.

This was, in effect, the ancient world's postal system. And like any good postal system, it served multiple purposes simultaneously. It allowed the king to issue orders and receive reports with unprecedented speed. It facilitated the movement of troops and supplies along a known, maintained route. And it enabled merchants to move goods across the empire with greater safety and reliability than they could have managed on unmarked tracks.

Trade followed the road. So did culture. So did ideas. The Royal Road was not simply a logistical tool - it was the connective tissue of an empire that might otherwise have fragmented into isolated regions with nothing in common but a shared king they rarely saw.

Economic Systems: Making the Empire Pay

An empire that cannot fund itself cannot survive. Cyrus understood that military conquest was only the beginning - the harder work was building an economy that generated enough surplus to pay armies, maintain roads, reward loyal governors, and project Persian power outward.

The satrap system served economic as well as administrative purposes. Each province was assessed a tribute - a fixed contribution of goods, silver, or both - that flowed upward to the imperial treasury. This was not random extraction. Different satrapies contributed according to their resources: some paid in silver, others in grain, timber, horses, or luxury goods. The system was calibrated to what each region could actually produce, which made it more sustainable than simple plunder.

Trade networks flourished under Persian rule, partly because the empire's sheer size created a vast internal market. Merchants moving goods along the Royal Road could travel through dozens of formerly separate kingdoms without crossing a hostile border. The relative stability of Persian governance - and the infrastructure that supported it - made long-distance commerce more viable than it had been under the fragmented political order that preceded the empire.

This economic integration was one of the less celebrated but deeply consequential achievements of Cyrus's reign. Prosperity, like stability, discouraged rebellion.

Pasargadae: A Capital Built to Impress

Power needs a face. For Cyrus, that face was Pasargadae - the capital city he founded in the heartland of Persia, in what is now the Fars province of modern Iran.

Pasargadae was more than an administrative center. It was a statement. Built on a broad plain surrounded by mountains, the city featured royal palaces, audience halls, and formal gardens - the famous Persian *pairidaeza*, from which the English word "paradise" ultimately derives. The layout of the complex was designed to project majesty: wide open spaces, monumental gateways, and structures that announced the wealth and ambition of the Achaemenid dynasty to any visitor who approached.

Cyrus's own tomb still stands at Pasargadae - a simple but striking stone structure raised on a stepped platform, modest in scale compared to the Egyptian pyramids but dignified in its restraint. Ancient sources record that Alexander the Great visited the tomb after his conquest of Persia and ordered it restored when he found it had been disturbed. Whether or not every detail of that account is accurate, the story captures something real: even Alexander, who had dismantled the Persian Empire, recognized Cyrus as a figure worth honoring.

Pasargadae represented the physical anchor of Persian identity - the place where the empire's founding story was written in stone and garden and silence.

What Historians Say

Administrative Evidence

Historians working on the Achaemenid period face a persistent challenge: much of what we know about Cyrus comes from sources written by people who were not Persian. Greek historians, Hebrew scripture, and Babylonian administrative records all offer glimpses of Cyrus's reign, but each carries its own perspective and its own gaps.

What the archaeological and documentary evidence does confirm is the basic architecture of the administrative system. Inscriptions, clay tablets, and the physical remains of road infrastructure support the broad picture of a satrapy-based empire with centralized oversight and regional flexibility. The satrap system was real, and it worked - the empire held together for two centuries after Cyrus's death, which is itself a form of evidence.

Historians also note that Cyrus's administrative innovations were not created from nothing. He drew on existing traditions in Mesopotamia and elsewhere, adapting and refining systems that had partial precedents in earlier empires. His achievement was synthesis and scale, not pure invention.

Later Developments Under Successors

Darius I, who ruled from 550 to 486 BCE, is often credited with formalizing and extending what Cyrus began. Under Darius, Aramaic became the official administrative language of the empire - a practical choice, since Aramaic was already widely understood across the Near East and could serve as a common tongue across dozens of different local languages. Darius also codified laws in Egypt and introduced other administrative reforms that tightened central authority without abandoning the flexible, culturally tolerant approach that Cyrus had established.

This continuity matters. The fact that Darius built on Cyrus's framework rather than replacing it suggests that the original system was sound. Successors who inherit broken systems tend to rebuild from scratch. Darius refined - which is a different kind of tribute.

What It Means

The Blueprint of Empire

Cyrus's administrative legacy is difficult to overstate. The satrapy system, the Royal Road, the economic integration of diverse provinces, the policy of cultural tolerance - taken together, these constituted something genuinely new in the ancient world: a model for governing large, diverse populations without relying primarily on terror or forced assimilation.

Later empires studied this model, consciously or not. Alexander the Great, after conquering Persia, retained the satrapy system rather than dismantling it - a telling sign that he recognized its effectiveness. The Roman Empire's provincial system bears structural resemblances to the Persian approach. The basic logic - delegate authority, maintain oversight, allow local variation within imperial limits - has recurred in one form or another across centuries of imperial history.

Cyrus did not invent empire. But he may have invented the administrative grammar that made large empires governable over the long term.

Leadership Lessons

What made Cyrus effective as a ruler was not simply military genius, though he had that. It was a quality rarer among conquerors: the ability to think about governance as a system rather than a personal performance.

Many ancient rulers held their empires together through the force of their own personality - and watched those empires fracture the moment they died. Cyrus built institutions. He created structures that could function without him, that could absorb his death and continue operating. The empire he founded outlasted him by two centuries precisely because it did not depend on any single person to keep it running.

Consider, too, his approach to the people he conquered. Cyrus did not demand that Babylonians become Persians, or that Lydians abandon their gods. He asked for loyalty and tribute, and in return he offered protection and a degree of autonomy. This was not sentimentality - it was political intelligence of a high order. An empire that governs with the grain of its subjects' identities is more stable than one that governs against it.

- Cyrus the Great ruled the Achaemenid Empire from approximately 576 to 530 BCE, building the largest empire the ancient world had yet seen.

- The satrapy system divided the empire into provinces governed by appointed regional governors called satraps, balancing local authority with central oversight.

- Royal inspectors - the "eyes and ears of the king" - monitored satraps and reported back to the center, preventing unchecked regional power.

- The Royal Road connected Sardis to Susa across roughly 2,700 kilometers, enabling rapid communication through a relay system of couriers and fresh horses.

- Economic integration across the empire, including standardized tribute and expanded trade networks, made Persian rule financially sustainable.

- Pasargadae, Cyrus's capital city, served as the physical and symbolic heart of the Achaemenid Empire, featuring royal palaces, formal gardens, and Cyrus's own tomb.

- Darius I extended and formalized Cyrus's administrative innovations, establishing Aramaic as the official imperial language and codifying laws across the empire.

- Cyrus's model - delegate, oversee, tolerate - became a template that later empires, including Alexander's and Rome's, would draw upon in their own governance.

Cyrus died in battle in 530 BCE, somewhere on the empire's northeastern frontier. He left behind no single successor who matched his combination of military skill and administrative vision - but he left behind something more durable: a system that could run without him. The empire he founded would endure for another two centuries, a living argument that the truest measure of a ruler lies not in what they accomplish in their lifetime, but in what they build that survives it.

Chapter 9
The Mystery of His Death

A queen plunges the severed head of the world's most powerful king into a skin filled with human blood. "Drink your fill," she says, "since you thirsted for blood." It is one of the most vivid death scenes in all of ancient history - and it may never have happened at all.

The death of Cyrus the Great, founder of the Achaemenid Empire and conqueror of half the known world, remains one of antiquity's most compelling unsolved mysteries. He died around 530 BCE, somewhere in the vast steppe lands beyond the eastern edges of his empire, during a campaign against a nomadic people called the Massagetae. That much is broadly agreed upon. Everything else - the battle, the defeat, the manner of his death - survives only through the accounts of Greek writers who were not there, who wrote decades after the fact, and who had their own reasons for telling the story the way they did.

What follows is the story of Cyrus's final campaign: what we know, what we think we know, and why the gap between those two things matters.

The Final Push Eastward

By the time Cyrus turned his attention to the northeastern frontier of his empire, he had already accomplished what no ruler before him had managed. He had toppled Lydia, absorbed Babylon, and built an empire stretching from the Aegean coast to the edge of the Iranian plateau. His reign had lasted more than two decades. He was, by any measure, at the height of his power.

And yet he kept moving.

The Massagetae occupied the steppe regions of what is now roughly Kazakhstan and Uzbekistan - open, unforgiving terrain that bore no resemblance to the walled cities Cyrus had spent his career capturing. These were not a sedentary people who could be besieged. They were nomadic warriors, expert riders, and fierce fighters who had no cities to lose and no fixed territory to defend. Campaigning against them required a completely different kind of war.

Why Cyrus chose to fight them at all is a question worth pausing on. Historical sources suggest he initially attempted diplomacy, approaching Tomyris - the queen who led the Massagetae - with a proposal of political alliance through marriage. She rejected it. Whether Cyrus genuinely sought peace or whether the marriage proposal was a calculated move to absorb her people into his empire without bloodshed, we cannot say with certainty. What is clear is that when diplomacy failed, he chose war.

War Against the Massagetae

Tomyris was not a figure to be underestimated. She ruled her people with evident authority, and when Cyrus's armies crossed into Massagetae territory, she met the threat directly. Ancient sources describe her warning Cyrus to turn back - a warning he ignored.

What followed was a major battle, the details of which differ depending on which ancient source you consult. Herodotus, writing in the fifth century BCE, describes a two-stage conflict. In the first engagement, a Persian force lured a Massagetae detachment - led by Tomyris's son, Spargapises - into a trap. The Persians set out a feast, allowed the Massagetae warriors to eat and drink themselves into a stupor, and then attacked. Spargapises was captured. When he regained his senses and grasped what had happened, he took his own life.

Tomyris, according to Herodotus, was furious. She sent a message to Cyrus: give back her son, or she would give him more blood than he could drink. Cyrus did not comply. The second battle was far larger and far more brutal - Herodotus calls it the fiercest battle ever fought between non-Greek peoples. And at the end of it, Cyrus was dead.

The Death of Cyrus

Here is where the accounts diverge, and where history shades into legend.

Herodotus tells us that Cyrus was killed in the battle itself, his army largely destroyed. Tomyris then found his body among the dead, filled a wineskin with human blood, and submerged his head in it - her grim fulfillment of the promise she had made. It is a scene of raw, almost theatrical vengeance, and Herodotus presents it as the fitting end of a man who had grown too ambitious, too hungry for conquest.

Xenophon, the other major Greek source on Cyrus, tells a completely different story. In his *Cyropaedia* - a work that is more philosophical novel than strict history - Cyrus dies peacefully in his bed, surrounded by his sons, dispensing final wisdom like a philosopher-king. There is no battle with the Massagetae in Xenophon's telling, no Tomyris, no wineskin of blood. Cyrus simply grows old, reflects on his life, and dies with dignity.

These two versions could hardly be more different. One ends in battlefield defeat and posthumous humiliation. The other ends in serene, almost Socratic acceptance. Both were written by Greeks. Neither was written by a Persian.

What Historians Say

Herodotus and the Problem of Distance

Herodotus is the most detailed source we have for Cyrus's death, and he was honest enough to acknowledge his own uncertainty. He notes that several accounts of Cyrus's end were circulating in his time and that he chose to present the one he found most credible - the battle with the Massagetae and the death at Tomyris's hands. That admission of selectivity is both admirable and revealing. Herodotus was writing roughly half a century after the events he described, drawing on oral traditions and secondhand reports. His account is vivid and internally coherent, but it is not eyewitness testimony.

There is also the question of narrative purpose. Herodotus was deeply interested in the theme of overreach - the idea that great rulers who push too far eventually fall. Cyrus's death at the hands of a woman he had tried to manipulate through a marriage proposal fits that moral framework almost too neatly. That doesn't make it false. But it does mean we should read it with some awareness of the lens through which it was written.

Xenophon and the Idealized King

Xenophon's *Cyropaedia* presents an even more obvious interpretive challenge. He was not writing history in any modern sense - he was writing a portrait of ideal leadership, using Cyrus as his model. His peaceful deathbed scene tells us a great deal about what Xenophon believed a great ruler should be, and rather less about what actually happened in 530 BCE. Scholars treat the *Cyropaedia* as a valuable philosophical text, but not as a reliable chronicle of events.

Other Accounts and the Silence of Persian Sources

Beyond Herodotus and Xenophon, a handful of other ancient writers mention Cyrus's death, though none add significant new detail. What is most striking - and most limiting - is the complete absence of Persian sources from the period. No contemporary Persian text describing Cyrus's final campaign has survived. Achaemenid inscriptions that do survive focus on royal achievements, not defeats. Later Persian kings, including Artaxerxes, had their own political reasons for shaping how Cyrus was remembered, which means even the Persian tradition around his memory may have been curated long after the fact.

What It Means

The Most Likely Scenario

Stripped of its most dramatic elements, the core of Herodotus's account is probably closer to the truth than Xenophon's idealized alternative. Cyrus almost certainly died during a military campaign in the northeastern steppe, most likely in conflict with the Massagetae or a people in that region. His body was reportedly returned to Persia - his tomb at Pasargadae, which still stands, was a genuine site of royal veneration in the ancient world. That detail suggests his remains were recovered and treated with appropriate ceremony, consistent with a battlefield death rather than a peaceful end far from home.

The more theatrical elements - Tomyris's speech, the wineskin of blood - are harder to evaluate. They may reflect genuine oral traditions that circulated among the peoples of the steppe. They may be Greek embellishments. They may be both: a kernel of real event dressed in the storytelling conventions of the ancient world.

Why the Truth Is Uncertain

What makes Cyrus's death genuinely difficult to pin down is not just the passage of time. It is the nature of the sources themselves. Greek writers were working from oral traditions, translated accounts, and their own cultural assumptions. Persian sources were shaped by the political needs of subsequent dynasties. The Massagetae left no written records at all. Every account of what happened in that steppe battle in 530 BCE is filtered through at least one layer of interpretation, and usually more.

Historians differ on how much weight to give Herodotus's version, and the debate is unlikely to be resolved without new archaeological evidence - which, given the terrain and the nomadic nature of the

Massagetae, may never emerge. The honest position is that we know Cyrus died on campaign in the northeast, probably in battle, and that his death marked the end of an era. The rest is a story told by people who weren't there, about a man whose life had already become legend before his body was cold.

- Cyrus the Great died around 530 BCE during a campaign against the Massagetae, a nomadic people in the steppe regions of modern-day Central Asia.

- His opponent was Queen Tomyris, who rejected his diplomatic overtures and led her people against his army.

- Herodotus provides the most detailed account: a two-stage conflict ending in Cyrus's death and a dramatic act of posthumous vengeance by Tomyris.

- Xenophon's version, in which Cyrus dies peacefully in his bed, is considered by most historians to be a philosophical idealization rather than historical record.

- No Persian texts from the period describing the campaign have survived, leaving Greek accounts as the primary - and deeply imperfect - sources.

- Later political interests, including those of subsequent Persian kings, may have shaped how Cyrus's death was remembered and recorded.

- Most historians believe Cyrus died in battle in the northeast, but the specific details of his death remain genuinely uncertain.

The tomb of Cyrus still stands at Pasargadae, a simple stone structure that has outlasted nearly every empire built since his own. Ancient visitors, including Alexander the Great, came to pay their respects to the man buried there. Whatever the precise circumstances of his death - whether he fell in the chaos of a steppe battle or was found among the slain by a vengeful queen - the fact of his tomb reminds us that his people brought him home. He had built something worth mourning. What came next - the empire he left behind, and the sons who would fight over it - is a story shaped entirely by the world he made.

Chapter 10
The Tomb and the Message

A conqueror who built one of the ancient world's greatest cities never got to see it finished. Alexander the Great died in Babylon in 323 BC, far from the empire he had spent his life assembling - and what happened to his body afterward became one of history's most enduring puzzles.

The question of Alexander's tomb is not merely a matter of archaeology. It cuts to the heart of how power works, how legends are made, and how the dead can be made to speak on behalf of the living. For centuries, rulers, generals, and emperors made pilgrimages to wherever Alexander's remains were kept - not out of simple curiosity but because proximity to Alexander meant something. It conferred legitimacy. It announced ambition. It said, in the clearest possible terms: *I am the heir to something larger than myself.*

What follows traces Alexander's body from death to disappearance - through the political maneuvering that shaped where he was buried, the symbolism embedded in his tomb, and the remarkable moment when Julius Caesar stood before his remains and wept. Along the way, it asks what we actually know, what we only think we know, and why the mystery of his final resting place still captivates scholars today.

The Story

A Body Becomes a Prize

When Alexander died in Babylon, the struggle over his empire began almost immediately. His generals - the *Diadochi*, or "successors" - carved up his conquests with ruthless efficiency. But one prize stood apart from territory or treasure: the body of Alexander himself.

Ptolemy, one of Alexander's most trusted generals and the future ruler of Egypt, seized the body while it was being transported back to Macedonia for burial. He rerouted it to Egypt - first to Memphis, the ancient capital, and then, sometime in the late 4th or early 3rd century BC, to Alexandria, the city Alexander had founded on the Mediterranean coast. It was Ptolemy Philadelphus, Ptolemy's son and successor, who completed the transfer to Alexandria, placing the body in a tomb that would become one of the most visited sites in the ancient world.

This was not sentiment. Controlling Alexander's remains was a political act of the highest order. Whoever held the body held a kind of symbolic authority over Alexander's legacy - and in the fractured world of the successor kingdoms, that legacy was worth fighting for.

The Tomb in Alexandria

Alexandria in its prime was a city designed to dazzle. Its famous lighthouse, the Pharos, was one of the Seven Wonders of the Ancient World. Its library held hundreds of thousands of scrolls. And at the city's center stood the *Soma* - the tomb complex that housed Alexander's remains.

Ancient sources describe a structure of considerable grandeur, though the precise details vary. What is consistent across accounts is the impression it made: this was not a modest grave but a monument built to project permanence and power. Alexander's body was reportedly displayed in a golden or glass sarcophagus, visible to those who came to pay their respects. The tomb sat within a royal quarter of the city, surrounded by the graves of the Ptolemaic rulers who had chosen to be buried near him - as if proximity to Alexander in death might confer some of the same authority it had in life.

The symbolism was deliberate. Alexandria was Alexander's city, and the tomb was its beating heart. Pilgrims, rulers, and scholars came from across the Mediterranean world. To visit was to acknowledge the city's claim as the center of civilized power.

Caesar at the Tomb

Few moments in ancient history carry quite the charge of Julius Caesar's visit to Alexander's tomb in 48 BC. Caesar had just arrived in Egypt in pursuit of his rival Pompey, only to find that Pompey had already been murdered on the orders of the young pharaoh Ptolemy XIII. Egypt was in the middle of a civil war, and Caesar - himself in the middle of one - had landed in a city on the edge.

Yet he went to the tomb.

Ancient accounts record that Caesar wept when he stood before Alexander's remains. He was, at the time, around 52 years old - roughly the age at which Alexander had already been dead for nearly three decades. The contrast was not lost on him. Alexander had conquered the known world before he turned 33. Caesar, for all his achievements, was still fighting for supremacy in Rome.

The visit was personal, but it was also political theater. By standing at Alexander's tomb, Caesar placed himself in a lineage of greatness. He was not just a Roman general; he was a man who measured himself against the greatest conqueror who had ever lived. Other rulers followed the same pattern - Augustus Caesar reportedly visited the tomb as well, and ancient sources suggest he accidentally broke off part of Alexander's nose while leaning in to pay his respects.

The tomb, in other words, was not a passive monument. It was a stage.

What Historians Say

The Archaeological Evidence

Here is where the story turns genuinely mysterious: no one knows where Alexander's tomb is today.

Alexandria has been continuously inhabited for more than two thousand years, and the ancient city lies largely beneath the modern one. Excavations have been limited, complicated by the water table, urban infrastructure, and the sheer density of history layered beneath the streets. Dozens of sites have been proposed over the decades, and none has produced conclusive evidence.

What archaeology has confirmed is that Alexandria was indeed a city of extraordinary monuments and that a royal quarter existed in roughly the area ancient sources describe. But the *Soma* itself - if it still exists in any recognizable form - has not been found.

The Historical Accounts

Ancient writers, including Strabo and Diodorus Siculus, mention the tomb and describe it in enough detail to confirm its existence and general location within Alexandria. Their accounts are consistent in placing it at the city's center, near the intersection of its two main avenues.

What happened after the 4th century AD is murkier. The historian Leo the African documented the state of the tomb in the Middle Ages, by which point its condition had apparently deteriorated significantly. More provocatively, the historian Andrew Chugg has proposed that in 392 AD - as Christianity became the dominant religion of the Roman Empire - Alexander's tomb may have been converted into a Christian church, and his remains quietly rebranded as those of Saint Mark the Evangelist. The theory is contested, but it points to a broader historical pattern: sacred sites and sacred relics have a way of being repurposed when the culture around them shifts.

Historians differ on whether Chugg's hypothesis is plausible or overstated, but the underlying observation is sound. Empires change. Religions change. What endures is the human need for a physical site of veneration - and the willingness to adapt that site to new purposes.

What It Means

The Meaning of Simplicity

There is something quietly remarkable about the fact that Alexander - a man who conquered territories stretching from Greece to the edges of India, who founded cities across three continents, who was worshipped as a god in his own lifetime - ended up as a body in a box that people came to stare at.

The tomb's power did not come from military force or political decree. It came from what it represented: the idea that greatness leaves a mark, that the physical remains of an extraordinary life carry meaning beyond the life itself. Rulers who visited were not worshipping Alexander exactly - they were borrowing his aura, wrapping themselves in the reflected light of his legend.

That is a very human impulse. And it says as much about the visitors as it does about the man they came to see.

Legacy in Stone

Alexander's tomb, wherever it lies, is a monument to the strange persistence of historical memory. For centuries it functioned as a pilgrimage site, a political prop, and a symbol of civilizational ambition. Then it disappeared - swallowed by time, urban growth, religious transformation, or some combination of all three.

Its disappearance has, paradoxically, only deepened the legend. A tomb you can visit becomes a tourist attraction. A tomb you cannot find becomes a mystery - and mysteries have a way of keeping their subjects alive in the imagination far longer than any monument could.

Alexander has been dead for more than two thousand years. His tomb has been lost for at least a thousand. And yet the search continues, because the idea of finding it - of standing where Caesar stood, of looking at what Caesar saw - still carries weight. That is the real legacy in stone: not the structure itself, but the hunger it created.

- Alexander's body was seized by Ptolemy after his death in 323 BC and eventually transferred to Alexandria by Ptolemy Philadelphus.

- The tomb, known as the *Soma*, occupied a royal quarter of Alexandria and reportedly displayed Alexander's body in a golden or glass sarcophagus.

- Julius Caesar visited the tomb in 48 BC, reportedly weeping at the sight of Alexander's remains - a moment as much political statement as personal reflection.

- Ancient writers including Strabo and Diodorus Siculus confirm the tomb's existence and central location in Alexandria.

- No physical trace of the tomb has been conclusively identified by modern archaeology.

- Historian Andrew Chugg has proposed that Alexander's remains may have been rebranded as Saint Mark the Evangelist around 392 AD, though this theory remains debated.

- The tomb's disappearance has amplified rather than diminished Alexander's legend, turning a physical monument into an enduring historical mystery.

Alexander's power did not end with his death - it transformed. The man became a symbol, the symbol became a site, and the site became a story that outlasted the stone. Whatever lies beneath the streets of modern Alexandria, the search for it is itself a testament to how deeply one life can imprint itself on the centuries that follow.

Chapter 11
The Legacy That Outlived Empires

Empires die. Their armies scatter, their capitals crumble, their languages fade into silence. And yet something of Cyrus the Great has refused to disappear - not just for decades after his death in 530 BC, but for two and a half millennia. A Persian king who lived before Alexander, before the Roman Republic had found its footing, before the New Testament existed, is still cited today by politicians, philosophers, and human rights advocates. That kind of staying power demands an explanation.

Cyrus the Great founded the Achaemenid Empire and conquered Babylon in 539 BC, but those facts alone don't account for his endurance in human memory. What made Cyrus remarkable - and what makes him worth studying now - was not merely the size of what he built, but the manner in which he built it. His policies of religious tolerance, cultural restoration, and administrative sophistication set a template that later civilizations would return to again and again, often without fully realizing they were doing so. His legacy is not a relic. It is a living argument about how power can be exercised.

The Story

Immediate Successors: What Cyrus Left Behind

When Cyrus died around 530 BC, he left behind something far more difficult to inherit than territory: a governing philosophy. The Achaemenid Empire he founded was vast - stretching from the Aegean coast to the edges of Central Asia - but its real achievement was administrative. Cyrus had demonstrated that an empire could hold together not through constant military suppression, but through a degree of local autonomy, religious respect, and cultural accommodation that his contemporaries had largely abandoned.

His immediate successors faced the challenge of maintaining that balance while continuing to expand. The empire did continue to grow under rulers like Cambyses II and later Darius the Great, who formalized and extended many of the administrative structures Cyrus had pioneered. Darius in particular built on the foundation Cyrus had laid, organizing the empire into satrapies - regional provinces governed by appointed officials - and developing the road networks and communication systems that held such a sprawling domain together.

But the spirit of Cyrus's approach was harder to replicate than the structures. His personal engagement with conquered peoples, his willingness to participate in local religious ceremonies, his deliberate framing of himself not as a conqueror but as a liberator - these were qualities of character and political instinct, not simply policy. Later Achaemenid rulers would sometimes honor that tradition and sometimes abandon it. The empire endured for two more centuries after Cyrus, eventually falling to Alexander the Great in 330 BC, but the administrative and cultural framework Cyrus established shaped every decade of that span.

Perhaps most concretely, his decision following the conquest of Babylon in 539 BC to allow the Jewish exiles to return to Jerusalem and to restore their religious institutions left an immediate and documented mark on history. The Hebrew Bible records this in terms of profound gratitude, describing Cyrus in the book of Isaiah as a figure anointed by God - an extraordinary designation for a foreign, non-Jewish king. The communities he allowed to return home carried that memory with them, and it would echo through centuries of religious tradition.

Influence on Later Empires: A Template for Power

Alexander the Great conquered the Achaemenid Empire, but he did not simply erase it. He studied it. Ancient sources suggest that Alexander deliberately modeled aspects of his own imperial behavior on Cyrus, whom he admired deeply. When Alexander visited the tomb of Cyrus at Pasargadae, he reportedly found it desecrated and ordered it restored - a gesture that spoke to how seriously he took the Persian king's legacy. Alexander adopted Persian court customs, administrative practices, and even elements of royal dress, partly as a practical strategy for governing Persian subjects, but also as a conscious act of homage to a predecessor he considered great.

Rome, too, absorbed lessons from the Achaemenid model, though often indirectly. The Roman approach to provincial governance - allowing local customs and religions to persist so long as political loyalty was maintained - bore a structural resemblance to the system Cyrus had pioneered. Whether Roman administrators consciously drew on Persian precedent or arrived at similar conclusions through their own experience, the parallel is striking.

The influence extended further still. When Islamic civilization expanded rapidly in the seventh and eighth centuries AD, Persian administrative traditions - many of which traced their roots to the Achaemenid period - were absorbed into the new caliphates. Persian bureaucratic culture, literary traditions, and concepts of governance became foundational to Islamic imperial administration. The thread connecting these later empires to Cyrus is not always direct or acknowledged, but it runs through the history of statecraft in a way that historians have increasingly recognized.

What Cyrus had demonstrated, in essence, was that diversity within an empire need not be a source of weakness. Managed with intelligence and a degree of genuine respect, it could be a source of stability. That idea proved durable precisely because it worked.

Cultural and Religious Impact: Memory Carved in Clay

In 1879, archaeologists excavating the ruins of Babylon unearthed a small clay cylinder covered in cuneiform script. The Cyrus Cylinder, as it came to be known, recorded in Cyrus's own voice - or at least in the voice of his scribes - his account of the conquest of Babylon and his policies toward its people. He described restoring gods to their sanctuaries, allowing displaced populations to return to their homelands, and presenting himself as a ruler chosen by the Babylonian god Marduk to bring justice and order.

The discovery corroborated what biblical texts had long claimed about Cyrus's character and policies. For scholars and religious communities alike, it was a remarkable moment of convergence between archaeological evidence and ancient scripture. The cylinder became one of the most discussed artifacts in the history of the ancient world, and its text has been invoked - sometimes controversially - as an early declaration of human rights.

That interpretation requires care. The Cyrus Cylinder was a piece of royal propaganda as much as a policy document, crafted to legitimize Cyrus's rule in Babylonian terms. But even accounting for its political purpose, the substance of what it describes - religious restoration, the return of exiled peoples, the rejection of forced labor - reflected genuine policies that had real consequences for real people. The Jews who returned to Jerusalem were not a metaphor. The temples that were rebuilt were not rhetorical flourishes.

Across Jewish, Christian, and later Islamic traditions, Cyrus occupied a unique position: the foreign ruler who served divine purposes without belonging to the faith community he served. That theological significance kept his name alive in religious memory long after the political circumstances that produced it had vanished.

What Historians Say

Interpretations Across Time

Herodotus, writing in the fifth century BC, called Cyrus the "Father" of the Persian Empire - a title that captured both his foundational role and the affection his subjects reportedly bore him. But Herodotus was also a storyteller as much as a historian, and his account of Cyrus blends verifiable history with legend. The Cyrus of Herodotus is partly a literary figure: the wise king whose rise from obscurity to greatness follows the arc of a hero's journey.

For centuries, that heroic image dominated Western perceptions. Renaissance scholars and Enlightenment thinkers who read Xenophon's *Cyropaedia* - a philosophical biography of Cyrus written in the fourth century BC - encountered a portrait of the ideal ruler: just, moderate, capable of inspiring loyalty rather than merely demanding it. Xenophon's Cyrus was explicitly a model for how a leader should behave, and the text was widely read and admired by figures including Thomas Jefferson, who owned multiple copies.

This long tradition of idealization means that Cyrus has sometimes been more useful as a symbol than as a historical subject. The real Cyrus - a conqueror who waged wars, who died on a military campaign, whose empire was built through force as well as diplomacy - has occasionally been obscured by the legend.

Modern Views: Reassessing the Record

Contemporary historians approach Cyrus with greater precision. They acknowledge his genuine achievements while recognizing the propagandistic dimensions of the sources that celebrate him. The Cyrus Cylinder, for instance, is now understood as a document that followed established Mesopotamian conventions for royal legitimacy - Cyrus was presenting himself in terms his Babylonian subjects would recognize and accept. That doesn't make his policies fictional, but it does complicate the idea of him as a uniquely enlightened ruler acting from pure principle.

Modern scholarship also situates Cyrus more firmly within his historical context, recognizing that his policies of religious tolerance, while remarkable in their consistency and scope, were not entirely without precedent in the ancient Near East. What distinguished Cyrus was the scale and deliberateness with which he applied these principles across a vast and diverse empire. Historians today tend to see him as a politically sophisticated ruler whose genuine pragmatism and more idealistic impulses are difficult to fully separate - and perhaps were never fully separate in his own mind.

What It Means

Why Cyrus Is Still Admired

There is something almost paradoxical about the endurance of Cyrus's reputation. He was a conqueror. He built his empire through military campaigns that brought death and displacement. And yet he is remembered - across cultures, across faiths, across millennia - as a figure of justice and liberation. How does that happen?

Part of the answer lies in contrast. The rulers Cyrus displaced, particularly the Neo-Babylonian kings like Nabonidus and Belshazzar, had reputations for neglecting their people's religious needs and ruling with contemptuous indifference. Against that backdrop, Cyrus's policies of restoration and respect appeared genuinely transformative to those who experienced them. The Jewish exiles in Babylon had lived under rulers who had destroyed their temple and severed them from their homeland. Cyrus gave them permission to go home. That act of permission, whatever its political motivations, carried enormous human weight.

But contrast alone doesn't explain two and a half thousand years of admiration. What has kept Cyrus relevant is the idea he embodied - that power exercised with restraint and respect for human dignity is not only morally preferable but practically effective. That idea has never gone out of fashion, because the temptation to exercise power without restraint has never gone away. Every generation finds in Cyrus a useful argument.

His Place in World History

Cyrus the Great occupies a rare position in the historical record: a figure whose significance is acknowledged across traditions that rarely agree on anything. He appears in the Hebrew Bible as an instrument of divine will. He appears in Greek historical writing as the exemplary ruler. He appears in modern human rights discourse as an early advocate for the dignity of conquered peoples. That breadth of recognition is itself a historical fact worth taking seriously.

His place in world history rests on several foundations. He founded the first empire to govern successfully across genuinely diverse populations at massive scale. He established administrative practices that influenced every major empire that followed in the region. He demonstrated, through the concrete evidence of the Cyrus Cylinder and the biblical record, that a policy of cultural and religious accommodation could be both principled and effective. And he left behind a legend powerful enough to shape the thinking of leaders and philosophers for centuries after his death.

None of this makes Cyrus a saint. History rarely produces saints, and the ones it does produce are usually more complicated up close. But it does make him something arguably more interesting: a ruler whose legacy survived not because his empire survived, but because the ideas embedded in how he governed proved more durable than any territory he conquered.

Quick Summary

- Cyrus the Great founded the Achaemenid Empire and died around 530 BC, leaving behind both a vast territory and a governing philosophy built on tolerance and cultural accommodation.

- His immediate successors, including Darius the Great, extended and formalized the administrative structures Cyrus pioneered, including the satrapy system that held the empire together for two more centuries.

- Alexander the Great admired Cyrus deeply, studied his methods, and consciously modeled aspects of his own imperial behavior on the Persian king's example.

- Persian administrative traditions rooted in the Achaemenid period were absorbed into Islamic civilization, extending Cyrus's indirect influence far beyond the ancient world.

- The Cyrus Cylinder, discovered in 1879, provided archaeological corroboration of biblical accounts of Cyrus's policies and became one of the most discussed artifacts in ancient history.

- Herodotus called Cyrus the "Father" of the Persian Empire; Xenophon's *Cyropaedia* presented him as the model of ideal rulership and was widely read by Enlightenment thinkers including Thomas Jefferson.

- Modern historians recognize Cyrus as a politically sophisticated ruler whose tolerance was both genuinely principled and strategically effective, while acknowledging the propagandistic dimensions of the sources that celebrate him.

- His enduring legacy rests on the idea that power exercised with restraint and respect for human dignity is not only morally preferable but practically durable.

Cyrus built an empire, but empires end. What he also built - almost incidentally, through the accumulation of specific decisions about how to treat the people he conquered - was a reputation that proved impossible to bury. Long after the Achaemenid court had fallen silent and the great roads of Persia had crumbled, his name continued to travel. That is the rarest kind of power: not the kind that compels obedience, but the kind that earns memory.

Chapter 12
Between Myth and History

He freed captive peoples, returned stolen gods to their temples, and ruled an empire stretching from the Aegean to the edges of Central Asia - all before the concept of human rights had a name. Or so the story goes.

Cyrus the Great is one of antiquity's most compelling figures, and also one of its most contested. He founded the Achaemenid Persian Empire around 550 BCE, conquered Babylon without a battle, and left behind a legacy so powerful that kings, prophets, and philosophers were still invoking his name centuries after his death. But separating the historical Cyrus from the mythologized one is no simple task. Every source that describes him - Persian, Babylonian, Hebrew, Greek - carries its own agenda, its own cultural lens, its own version of who this man was and what he represented.

That tension between myth and history is not a problem unique to Cyrus. It is the central challenge of reading the ancient world. But Cyrus makes for an unusually sharp case study, because the gap between what the sources say and what we can verify is both wide and deeply instructive. Understanding how to read him means understanding how to read antiquity itself - with curiosity, with skepticism, and with a willingness to hold uncertainty without abandoning the search for truth.

The Framework

What We Know

Some facts about Cyrus are as solid as ancient history gets. He lived approximately between 600 and 530 BCE. He founded the Achaemenid Empire, the first great Persian empire, around 550 BCE, after defeating the Median king and absorbing his kingdom. He went on to conquer Lydia in western Anatolia and then Babylon, the most powerful city in the ancient Near East. By the time of his death, he ruled the largest empire the world had yet seen.

Multiple independent sources confirm these broad strokes. The Nabonidus Chronicle - a Babylonian administrative document, not a literary glorification - records the fall of Babylon to Cyrus in factual, bureaucratic language. The Cyrus Cylinder, a clay artifact discovered in the ruins of Babylon, bears an inscription in Cyrus's own name describing his entry into the city and his policies toward its people. These are not legends. They are contemporary records, produced close to the events they describe, and they establish a reliable skeleton of fact.

We also know that Cyrus died around 530 BCE, likely during a military campaign against the Massagetae, a nomadic people living in the steppes beyond the eastern frontier of his empire. He did not die peacefully in a palace. He died in the field, as he had lived.

These are the anchors. Everything else requires more careful handling.

What Is Likely True

Beyond the confirmed core, a second tier of claims carries strong plausibility without absolute certainty. Cyrus almost certainly pursued a deliberate policy of religious and cultural tolerance in the territories he conquered. The Cyrus Cylinder describes him restoring cult statues to their original temples and allowing displaced peoples to return to their homelands - a sharp contrast to the deportation policies of the Assyrian and Babylonian empires that preceded him. The Hebrew Bible, in the Book of Isaiah and elsewhere, credits Cyrus with permitting the Jewish exiles in Babylon to return to Judah and rebuild their temple. This account aligns with what the Cylinder describes, and there is no strong reason to doubt its general accuracy, even if the biblical framing casts Cyrus in explicitly theological terms.

Cyrus was also, in all likelihood, a genuinely skilled military and political strategist. His rapid expansion across Media, Lydia, and Babylon within roughly two decades suggests not just military force but an ability to co-opt local elites, adapt to different political systems, and present himself credibly to very different audiences. He was, by all available evidence, a ruler who understood the power of perception.

What remains uncertain is the degree to which these policies were principled rather than pragmatic. Was Cyrus tolerant because he believed in human dignity, or because tolerance was simply the most efficient way to govern a vast, diverse empire? The sources do not give us a clear answer - and the question itself may be anachronistic.

What Is Legend

Then there is the Cyrus of legend. Herodotus, writing in the fifth century BCE, tells us that Cyrus was the grandson of the Median king Astyages, that his birth was preceded by ominous dreams, and that as an infant he was ordered killed but survived through the intervention of a herdsman and his wife. The story follows a pattern familiar from other ancient traditions - Moses in the bulrushes, Romulus and Remus - and almost certainly belongs to the realm of origin mythology rather than biography.

Xenophon, writing even later, produced the *Cyropaedia* - literally "the education of Cyrus" - a philosophical novel dressed as biography. His Cyrus is a paragon of leadership: wise, just, self-controlled, and beloved by all who serve him. Xenophon was not writing history. He was constructing an idealized portrait of what a great ruler should look like, using Cyrus as a vehicle for his own political philosophy.

These legendary elements are not worthless. They tell us something real - about how Cyrus was remembered, about the values his successors wanted to associate with him, about the cultural work his image was made to perform. But they cannot be treated as biographical fact.

Sources Explained

Primary Sources

The most reliable evidence for Cyrus comes from sources produced in his own time or close to it, by cultures that had direct contact with his rule.

The Cyrus Cylinder, dating to around 539 BCE, is the most famous. Inscribed in Babylonian cuneiform, it presents Cyrus as the chosen of Marduk, the chief Babylonian god, who selected him to restore order after the failures of the last Babylonian king, Nabonidus. The Cylinder describes Cyrus returning displaced peoples and their gods to their homelands, abolishing forced labor, and repairing temples. Modern scholars debate how much of this represents genuine policy versus royal propaganda - the Cylinder was, after all, a public document designed to legitimize Cyrus's rule to a Babylonian audience. But its basic claims align with other evidence, which lends them credibility.

The Nabonidus Chronicle offers a more neutral perspective. As a Babylonian administrative text, it records the fall of Babylon in 539 BCE with notable restraint, describing Cyrus's entry into the city as peaceful and his treatment of the population as respectful. Nabonidus himself, the last Babylonian king, is portrayed as having lost divine favor - a framing that served Cyrus's interests but also reflects genuine Babylonian discontent with Nabonidus's rule.

Biblical texts, particularly in Isaiah, Ezra, and Chronicles, provide a third independent source. They describe Cyrus in explicitly providential terms - as an instrument of God's will - but their account of his policies toward the Jewish exiles is consistent with what the Cylinder describes.

Greek Historians

Greek sources present a different kind of challenge. Herodotus, often called the father of history, wrote his *Histories* in the mid-fifth century BCE, roughly a generation after Cyrus's death. He had access to oral traditions, Persian informants, and earlier written accounts, but he also had a storyteller's instinct and a Greek audience's appetite for drama. His account of Cyrus's birth, rise, and death is vivid and compelling - and heavily shaped by narrative convention.

Xenophon's *Cyropaedia*, written in the early fourth century BCE, is even further removed from the historical Cyrus. Xenophon was a soldier and philosopher, not a chronicler, and his portrait of Cyrus is openly idealized. He was less interested in what Cyrus actually did than in what Cyrus represented as a model of leadership. The *Cyropaedia* proved enormously influential in antiquity and beyond - it shaped how Alexander the Great thought about kingship, and later how Renaissance thinkers imagined the ideal prince - but it tells us more about Greek political thought than about the Persian king himself.

Neither Herodotus nor Xenophon should be dismissed. They preserve traditions and details that no other source records. But they must be read critically, as products of their own time and culture, not transparent windows onto the past.

What It Means

How to Read Ancient History

Cyrus's story is a masterclass in the problems and possibilities of ancient historiography. No single source gives us the complete picture. Each one reflects the priorities, assumptions, and agendas of the culture that produced it. Babylonian sources want to show that

Cyrus was divinely chosen to restore their traditions. Hebrew sources want to show that God works through foreign kings to fulfill his promises. Greek sources want to show what ideal leadership looks like. None of them are simply reporting facts.

This does not mean ancient sources are useless. It means they require triangulation. When multiple independent sources - Babylonian, Hebrew, and Greek - agree on the broad outlines of Cyrus's behavior, that convergence carries real evidential weight. When only one source makes a dramatic claim, especially one that follows a familiar narrative pattern, skepticism is warranted.

Reading ancient history well means holding two things at once: genuine respect for what the sources preserve, and honest acknowledgment of what they cannot tell us. The goal is not certainty. It is the most accurate picture we can construct from the evidence available - and a clear-eyed understanding of where that picture blurs.

The Truth About Cyrus

So who was Cyrus, really? He was almost certainly a military genius and a political innovator - a ruler who understood that empire could be built on co-option as well as conquest. He was the founder of a political tradition that would shape the ancient world for two centuries, and whose echoes reached far beyond Persia's borders. He was remembered as a liberator by peoples as different as the Babylonians and the Jews, which suggests his policies had real effects on real lives.

He was also a product of his time - a conqueror who built his empire through war, who died on a military campaign, and whose tolerance, however genuine, served the practical interests of imperial stability. The Cyrus Cylinder is a remarkable document, but it is also a piece of royal propaganda. The man behind it was complex, as powerful figures always are.

What makes Cyrus enduringly significant is not just what he did, but what he was made to mean. He became a symbol - of enlightened rule, of religious tolerance, of the possibility that power and humanity are not mutually exclusive. Whether the historical Cyrus fully embodied those ideals is a question the evidence cannot definitively answer. But the fact that so many different cultures, across so many centuries, reached for his image when they wanted to articulate those ideals says something important about the world he left behind.

- Cyrus the Great lived approximately 600-530 BCE and founded the Achaemenid Persian Empire around 550 BCE.

- Confirmed facts include his conquests of Media, Lydia, and Babylon, and his death during a campaign against the Massagetae.

- The Cyrus Cylinder and Nabonidus Chronicle are the most reliable primary sources, though both carry propagandistic elements.

- Biblical texts independently corroborate Cyrus's policy of allowing exiled peoples to return to their homelands.

- Greek historians Herodotus and Xenophon offer vivid but heavily idealized portraits that reflect Greek values more than Persian reality.

- Cyrus's reputation for tolerance is plausible and broadly supported, but whether it was principled or pragmatic remains uncertain.

- Reading ancient history requires triangulating across sources, acknowledging their biases, and distinguishing between what is confirmed, what is probable, and what is legend.

Cyrus the Great died more than two and a half millennia ago, but the questions his story raises have never gone away. How do we separate the man from the myth? How do we read sources that were never designed to be neutral? How do we honor the past without being deceived by it? These are not just problems for historians. They are the fundamental challenges of trying to understand any world other than our own - and they will sharpen in the chapters ahead, as the empires Cyrus set in motion collide with new forces, new ambitions, and new ways of remembering who mattered and why.

Conclusion
The Model of a Just Ruler

What does it mean to rule well? Not merely to conquer, or to accumulate, or to hold power - but to wield it in a way that leaves the world genuinely better than you found it? Few rulers in the ancient world asked that question as seriously as Ashoka. Fewer still tried to answer it with their entire empire.

Born in 304 BCE and ascending to the Mauryan throne around 268 BCE, Ashoka inherited one of the most powerful states the ancient world had ever seen - a vast empire stretching across the Indian subcontinent, built by his grandfather Chandragupta Maurya through ambition, strategy, and force. Ashoka expanded it further, in the same tradition. Then something changed. And in that change, he became something rarer than a great conqueror: a ruler who tried to be good.

This final chapter draws together the threads of Ashoka's life and reign - his achievements, the lessons his leadership offers, and the enduring question of what his example means across the long arc of history.

A Summary of His Achievements

By any conventional measure, Ashoka's reign marked the peak of the Mauryan Empire. Politically, administratively, and geographically, the empire under his rule reached its greatest extent. But the achievements that outlasted his armies were not won on battlefields.

After his transformation - the moment when the devastation of the Kalinga war turned a conqueror toward conscience - Ashoka built something more durable than territory. He built a system of moral governance he called *Dhamma*: a framework rooted in Buddhist principles, emphasizing non-violence, compassion, religious tolerance, and the welfare of all living beings. This was not merely personal philosophy. He made it policy.

His edicts, carved into rock faces and stone pillars across the subcontinent, communicated directly with his subjects in their own languages. They announced the construction of roads, rest houses, and wells. They called on officials to treat people fairly. They urged tolerance between religious communities at a time when such tolerance was far from guaranteed. These were not monuments to his own glory. They were instructions for how a society should treat its people.

Ashoka also played a decisive role in spreading Buddhism beyond India's borders. Through missionaries, diplomatic envoys, and the example of his own court, Buddhist teachings reached Sri Lanka, Central Asia, and eventually much of the wider world. His son Mahinda and daughter Sanghamitta are credited with carrying the faith to Sri Lanka, where it took deep root. The religion that would shape the spiritual lives of hundreds of millions across Asia owes part of its global reach to Ashoka's deliberate patronage.

His cultural symbols proved equally enduring. The Ashoka Chakra - the wheel of *Dhamma* - sits at the center of the modern Indian national flag. The Lion Capital of Ashoka, originally erected at Sarnath, became the official emblem of the Republic of India. Few rulers from the ancient world have left their mark so visibly on a modern nation-state.

Leadership Lessons

What can a ruler who lived more than two thousand years ago teach about leadership? Quite a lot - not because his world resembles ours, but because the tensions he faced are timeless.

Power is not the same as authority. Ashoka had absolute power. He commanded armies, controlled trade routes, and governed millions.

But the authority he earned - the genuine respect and moral weight his reign carried - came not from force but from restraint. He chose, deliberately, to govern through persuasion rather than coercion after Kalinga. That choice is harder than it sounds. Power tends to expand. Choosing to limit it requires a quality rarer than courage: humility.

Accountability must be built into the system. Ashoka did not simply declare himself virtuous and expect his officials to follow suit. He created mechanisms - the *Dhamma Mahamattas*, officers specifically charged with promoting welfare and monitoring the treatment of subjects - to institutionalize his values. Good intentions at the top mean little without structures that carry those intentions downward through a vast bureaucracy. Leaders who rely on personal virtue alone, without building accountable systems, leave nothing behind when they are gone.

Communication is governance. His edicts were not decorative. They were functional. By inscribing policy in public places, in the languages people actually spoke, Ashoka treated his subjects as people who deserved to know how they were being governed and why. That instinct - that rulers owe their people transparency and explanation - was radical in the ancient world. It remains undervalued in many parts of the modern one.

Transformation is possible, but it must be genuine. Ashoka's shift from conqueror to moral ruler was not a political rebrand. It reshaped his policies, his priorities, and his personal conduct. History is skeptical of rulers who claim conversion while their behavior stays the same. Ashoka's edicts, his welfare programs, and his restraint in military expansion after Kalinga suggest his change was real. Genuine transformation in leadership is rare - and recognizable precisely because it costs something.

Moral vision requires institutional continuity. This is perhaps the hardest lesson. After Ashoka's death in 232 BCE, the Mauryan Empire fragmented. His successors could not or would not sustain what he had built. The *Dhamma* did not outlast the dynasty in any formal sense. His Buddhism spread; his governance model did not. A leader's greatest vulnerability is the gap between personal vision and institutional resilience. What cannot survive the founder rarely survives at all.

Final Reflection

Ashoka lived for thirty-six years after becoming emperor. He had time - more than most rulers get - to test his ideas against reality. And the reality was complicated. His empire was vast and difficult to govern. His moral ambitions sometimes collided with the practical demands of holding a state together. He was not a saint. He was a ruler who tried, seriously and at scale, to make justice the organizing principle of his power.

That attempt did not produce a perfect empire. No such thing exists. But it produced something more interesting: a record. The edicts survive. The Lion Capital stands. The Chakra turns at the center of a flag seen by over a billion people. Ashoka left behind not just ruins but evidence - evidence that a ruler once looked at the suffering his power had caused and decided to govern differently.

History offers few enough examples of that. The ones it does offer deserve to be taken seriously - not as myths, not as propaganda, but as genuine experiments in what leadership can be when it aims at something beyond the accumulation of power.

Ashoka's experiment ended. His empire fell. But the question he spent his reign trying to answer - what does it mean to rule justly? - has never stopped being asked. Every generation inherits it. Every leader, in every era, must decide whether to take it seriously.

Some do. Most don't. That is precisely why the ones who do still matter.

- Ashoka ruled the Mauryan Empire at its peak, from approximately 268 to 232 BCE, inheriting a dynasty founded by his grandfather Chandragupta Maurya.

- After the brutal conquest of Kalinga, he underwent a profound transformation and adopted Buddhist principles of non-violence and compassion as the basis of his rule.

- His policy of *Dhamma* emphasized moral governance, public welfare, religious tolerance, and the ethical treatment of all living beings - enforced through edicts and dedicated officials called *Dhamma Mahamattas*.

- Rock and pillar edicts, inscribed across the subcontinent in local languages, represent one of the earliest known examples of a ruler communicating policy directly and publicly to his subjects.

- He played a central role in spreading Buddhism beyond India, with missionaries reaching Sri Lanka and Central Asia during his reign.

- His cultural legacy endures in modern India: the Ashoka Chakra appears on the national flag, and the Lion Capital of Sarnath serves as the national emblem.

- After his death, the Mauryan Empire fragmented - a reminder that moral vision, however powerful, requires institutional foundations to outlast the individual who holds it.

The Ashoka Chakra still turns on the Indian flag, carried aloft at every state function and international summit. That a modern republic chose the symbol of a third-century BCE emperor as its emblem speaks to something durable in his vision - a conviction that power exists not to serve the ruler but the ruled. Whether any future leader will answer that conviction as fully as Ashoka attempted remains, as ever, an open question.

You've reached the end of this journey through the life and legacy of Cyrus the Great - and that's no small thing.

By now, you've followed his story from uncertain beginnings to the creation of one of history's most remarkable empires. You've seen how he rose, how he ruled, and why his name has endured for more than two thousand years. More importantly, you've explored the ideas behind his success - leadership, strategy, and a vision of power that was rare in the ancient world and still relevant today.

If you found this book valuable, insightful, or simply enjoyable to read, I'd greatly appreciate it if you could take a moment to leave a review. Reviews help other readers discover the book and decide if it's right for them - and they make a real difference.

Even a short review sharing your thoughts or what you found most interesting is incredibly helpful.

Thank you for reading, and for taking the time to explore the story of one of history's most fascinating figures.